Practical Guide to SAP® CO Templates

Tom King

Thank you for purchasing this book from Espresso Tutorials!

Like a cup of espresso coffee, Espresso Tutorials SAP books are concise and effective. We know that your time is valuable and we deliver information in a succinct and straightforward manner. It only takes our readers a short amount of time to consume SAP concepts. Our books are well recognized in the industry for leveraging tutorial-style instruction and videos to show you step by step how to successfully work with SAP.

Check out our YouTube channel to watch our videos at
https://www.youtube.com/user/EspressoTutorials.

If you are interested in SAP Finance and Controlling, join us at
http://www.fico-forum.com/forum2/
to get your SAP questions answered and contribute to discussions.

Related titles from Espresso Tutorials:

- ► Thomas Michael: Reporting for SAP® Asset Accounting
  http://5029.espresso-tutorials.com

- ► Tanya Duncan: Practical Guide to SAP® CO-PC (Product Cost Controlling) *http://5064.espresso-tutorials.com*

- ► Ashish Sampat: First Steps in SAP® Controlling (CO)
  http://5069.espresso-tutorials.com

- ► Rosana Fonseca: Practical Guide to SAP® Material Ledger (ML)
  http://5116.espresso-tutorials.com

- ► Marjorie Wright: Practical Guide to SAP® Internal Orders (CO-OM)
  http://5139.espresso-tutorials.com

- ► Ashish Sampat: Expert Tips to Unleash the Full Potential of SAP® Controlling *http://5140.espresso-tutorials.com*

- ► John Pringle: Practical Guide to SAP® Profit Center Accounting
  http://5144.espresso-tutorials.com

- ► Janet Salmon & Claus Wild: First Steps in SAP® S/4HANA Finance
  http://5149.espresso-tutorials.com

- ► Stefan Eifler, Christoph Theis: Value Flows into SAP® ERP FI, CO and CO-PA *http://5199.espresso-tutorials.com*

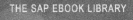

Tom King
Practical Guide to SAP® CO Templates

ISBN:	978-1-72170-693-8
Editor:	Karen Schoch
Cover Design:	Philip Esch
Cover Photo:	© salita2010, # 139145958 – stock.adobe.com
Interior Book Design:	Johann-Christian Hanke

All rights reserved.

1st Edition 2018

© 2018 by Espresso Tutorials GmbH, Gleichen 2018

URL: *www.espresso-tutorials.com*

Feedback
We greatly appreciate any kind of feedback you have concerning this book. Please mail us at *info@espresso-tutorials.com*.

Table of Contents

Foreword

One of the good things about working with SAP systems is the vast amount of information that is available through books and the internet. Unfortunately, this can also be a drawback. There is so much information available that it is sometimes difficult to find exactly what is needed to solve a particular problem. SAP does an excellent job of documenting the various modules, but often it is necessary to sift through the data to find exactly what is needed. By necessity, the information provided is more theoretical in nature and describes functions from a more technical point of view. The point necessary to enable a full understanding of how a certain transaction can be used may be buried and easily overlooked. Internet forums and blogs have provided an alternative means of finding out how experts have solved specific problems. As long as you know how to pose the question, you can learn a great deal about how transactions work and the configuration associated with making them work in a certain way. The big drawback here is that the information presented is disjointed and might almost, but not quite, solve a particular problem.

I have personally had these issues when looking for information on how my company could use CO templates. Our implementation consultants were able to guide the way, but I had to dig out many details myself. As we became more mature in our understanding of how SAP works, and we no longer needed consultants' help, the task of digging fell to us. What was needed was a "one-stop shop" that not only provided the details of how to set up templates, but also the uses for which they could be put to use. This book is the result of that wish: **A Practical Guide to Using CO Templates**. At the very least, I hope that this book takes the first step towards providing a single resource for anyone searching for the best way to implement templates in their implementation.

The book is structured to guide the reader through setting up and using CO templates for both plan and actual allocations. Chapter 1 provides a background of the many allocation methodologies provided by SAP, ending in Activity Based Costing and templates. Chapter 2 looks at a product costing scenario and walks through various template structures in order to orient the reader on the set-up and use of the templates. Chapter 3 takes the same scenario and applies it to actual allocations that occur as part of month-end closing procedures. The main technical thrust of the chapter is to show how to construct the various methods and formulas that are used to calculate the quantities to allocate. Chapter 4 takes a step back and looks at the configuration needed for templates, and gives a glimpse into how extensions can be created to make this an even more powerful tool. CO templates are used in a multitude of areas in Controlling. Chapter 5 provides a brief overview of how templates are processed in each of the various environments. The concept of allocating costs with templates was extended to Easy Cost Planning, which uses templates as its "derivation rules" for costing models. This subject can command a book of its own, covering not only how templates fit in to cost modeling, but also how to effectively use the cost models in various planning scenarios. Chapter 6 gives a brief overview of Easy Cost Planning, focusing on how templates are used to calculate costs. Finally, I have included an appendix in Chapter 7 which contains lists of items that I have found helpful in understanding how to use templates. If I have left anything out of these lists that may be important to you, I apologize up-front.

I want to thank several people who have helped me in writing this book. First of all, I want to give special thanks to Martin Munzel and especially Alice Adams of Espresso Tutorials for getting me to write the book in the first place. The experience has been great, and their help has been invaluable. Another important contributor is Karen Schoch, whose editing skills helped polish the manuscript and keep all my references straight. I would also like to thank John Jordan of ERPCorp whose yearly Controlling conference in San Diego was instrumental in connecting me with Martin and Alice. They organized a fantastic conference! There are many people at Milliken and Company who have been instrumental in encouraging me and helping me hone my skills; including Chip Ward, Curt Jarrell, Vim Patel, and others too numerous to name here. Milliken has fostered an environment that allows us to search for proper solutions within the confines of the SAP framework and has enabled me to expand my ERP knowledge. Finally, I want to thank my family, who have supported me in this endeavor, and especially my wife Cesily, who has been my first-line editor. One of the trials of being married to an English teacher is that it forces me to pay attention to the grammar!

We have added a few icons to highlight important information. These include:

Tips

Tips highlight information that provides more details about the subject being described and/or additional background information.

Examples

Examples help illustrate a topic better by relating it to real world scenarios.

Attention

Attention notices highlight information that you should be aware of when you go through the examples in this book on your own.

Finally, a note concerning the copyright: all screenshots printed in this book are the copyright of SAP SE. All rights are reserved by SAP SE. Copyright pertains to all SAP images in this publication. For the sake of simplicity, we do not mention this specifically underneath every screenshot.

1 Introduction to CO templates

SAP provides several methods for cost allocations in the Controlling module. Most of these methods use fairly simple calculations that can result in imprecise spreading of costs to receiver objects. With the development of the Activity Based Costing module, SAP introduced the concept of the template. The features of templates enable access to data, characteristics, and formulas to be used in the creation of complex calculations generating much more accurate allocations.

1.1 Cost allocation in SAP

The Controlling module (CO) in SAP is the means by which financial data is presented in a fashion which provides management with the information to measure the cost performance of the organization. To facilitate this process, cost-relevant data from the Financial module (FI) is assigned to CO objects such as cost centers, business processes, projects, orders, and profit centers. The method for posting these costs involves the use of cost elements. When cost object relevant financial accounts are posted in FI, the posting is replicated in CO with the costs posted to the object assigned in the original posting. Costs can be planned for the cost elements in the CO objects, allowing for a comparison between what was posted and what was planned. The Cost Center Accounting module (CO-CCA) is used to manage cost centers associated with specific operational responsibility. Costs planned and posted to cost centers enable managers to understand the performance of their departments. Another example of a CO module is Product Cost Controlling (CO-PC). The primary goal of this portion of Controlling is to understand the costs relating to the manufacturing process in order to provide the basis for determining the cost performance of the company's products. Similarly, other CO entities, such as Profitability Analysis, Internal Orders, and Project Systems, use the FI to CO connection to help manage various other aspects of the organization.

What is a cost element?

 A *cost element* identifies a type of cost posted in the CO module. Primary cost elements are associated with general ledger accounts, and the CO posting is tied directly to the financial posting in the FI module. Secondary cost elements are used for moving costs between cost objects in the CO module and are independent of primary general ledger postings. With the introduction of S/4HANA and the Universal Journal, secondary cost elements have themselves become accounts. However, the purpose of the secondary cost elements in S/4HANA has not changed from the earlier ERP versions.

Certain overhead costs cannot be directly assigned to a specific cost object because they might represent a service that is external to that cost object. A good example of this is the assignment of labor costs to a product. Planning labor costs directly to a product is extremely difficult. Posting and managing the costs directly at the product level would be almost impossible. Therefore, labor costs are normally planned to a cost center and assigned to an activity type. The activity type is used to allocate those costs from the cost center to the product.

The cost center is used to manage various costs that are related to an area of responsibility within the organization. In a similar manner to the product cost, certain overhead costs to be assigned to a cost center represent a service that is better managed in a separate overhead cost center. In that case, a portion of the cost in the overhead cost center is allocated back to the first cost center.

Indirect costs

 The Maintenance Department in a manufacturing facility services the equipment used on the production floor. The maintenance manager is responsible for the performance of that department and a cost center has been assigned for that purpose. Since it is important to include the maintenance costs as part of product costs, the costs incurred in this department must be allocated to the various production departments within the plant. This allocation accounts for the indirect cost of maintenance in the products.

SAP provides several methods for allocating both plan and actual costs between cost objects in Controlling. The main tools that are used include overhead costing sheets, activity type allocations, assessments, distributions, and template allocations.

1.1.1 Overhead costing sheets

One way to allocate costs from a cost center or business process to another cost object is to use overhead costing sheets. The costing sheet is basically a procedure that is set up to apply conditions (overhead rates) to base costs (ranges of cost elements). Each costing sheet contains four key elements which are used in the calculation and execution of the overhead allocation. These elements are assigned, in various combinations, to rows which define the rules of how overhead costs are assigned to the receiving cost object.

Row	Base	Overhead rate	Description	From	To	Credit
10	B000		Material			
20		C010	Freight cost	10	19	E01
30	B001		Labor			
40		C020	Fringes	30	39	E02
50		C030	Warehousing	10	49	E03

Figure 1.1: Overhead costing sheet

The 'base' provides a range of cost elements or origin groups which identify the cost elements used to calculate the overhead costs. The 'overhead rate' is a condition that defines percentages or amounts used in the calculation of the overhead to be applied to the accumulated costs in the assigned rows. The row range ('from'/'to') defines the rows to which the overhead rate applies. Looking at Figure 1.1, overhead rate C010 in row 20 is applied to rows 10 - 19 in the costing sheet. Because only row 10 is defined, C010 applies only to costs for cost elements assigned to base B000. Overhead rate C020 in row 40 only applies to the costs assigned to the base in row 30. However, C030, which is in row 50, is applied to the cumulative costs, including the overhead calculations for all the rows identified in the costing sheet. The fourth element is the 'credit key', which defines the sender cost object and secondary cost element used to post the allocation.

Figure 1.2 shows what happens when the overhead is allocated using the costing sheet. The allocation looks at the postings associated with the base cost elements and applies the overhead rates that have been defined. The amount calculated is assigned to the secondary cost element defined in the credit key, crediting the sender cost center and debiting the receiver cost object.

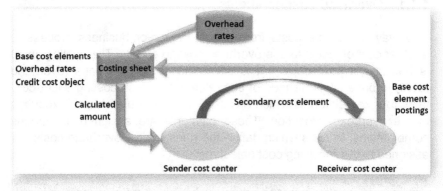

Figure 1.2: Cost allocation with overhead costing sheets

Overhead costing sheets can be a powerful tool for performing allocations and once the costing sheet is set up, the allocation is simple to perform. However, since the allocations are based strictly on financial postings and are limited to percentage calculations or fixed amounts, this method can end up smearing the overhead costs without regard to the true consumption of those costs.

1.1.2 Distributions

Distributions are a type of cost allocation that are primarily used for cost centers. A distribution is considered an indirect allocation, because the posting of an activity is not the basis for the allocation. Instead, user-defined factors are used to post the amounts in a cycle. These factors include percentage rates, amounts, statistical key figures, and even posted amounts as the basis for determining the allocation. A distribution is used to allocate primary costs using the original cost element. The original posting is made in the sender cost center. This cost is then re-posted (distributed) to the various receivers identified in a distribution cycle based on tracing factors and weighting factors defined in the cycle.

Tracing factors and weighting factors

 A *tracing factor* is a posting associated with a receiving cost object which can be used to help determine the amount of cost to be allocated or distributed from a sending cost object. Postings for activity type quantities, statistical key figure quantities, and cost postings can all be used as tracing factors. A *weighting factor* is used for calculating the amount associated with the tracing factor to be posted to a specific receiver object. The tracing factor quantity for each receiver is multiplied by the weighting factor. The weighted quantities for all the receivers are then added together. The amount to be distributed is divided by this result and posted to each receiver in proportion to the weighted quantity for that receiver.

Figure 1.3 shows how the distribution cycle works. The original posting of electricity is made in the energy cost center. The distribution cycle defines the rules as to how the original posting is to be distributed to the various receiver cost centers. The cycle credits the energy cost center using the original primary cost element (5100) and then reposts the costs to the receiver cost centers using the same primary cost element.

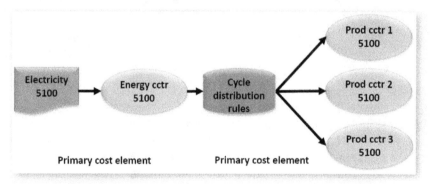

Figure 1.3: Distribution cycle

Distribution cycles can be used for both plan and actual postings and provide a repeatable way for reposting the primary costs. Distribution is easy to set up and use, and is very repeatable. However, the allocation method is fairly simplistic and may not accurately reflect the desired allocation of the costs.

1.1.3 Assessments

Assessments are similar to distributions. Instead of reposting the primary cost element to the receiver cost objects, an assessment first combines costs from multiple primary costs from a sender cost object and assigns these costs to a secondary cost element. Then, those grouped costs are allocated to various receivers using the tracing factors and weighting factors defined in an assessment cycle. Only the combined value of the secondary cost element is credited to the sender, and the original primary postings remain on the sender.

Figure 1.4 shows what happens in the assessment cycle. Postings have been made for electricity and natural gas in the energy cost center. The assessment cycle combines the costs for these postings and credits that amount to the sender cost center using a secondary cost element (4100). Each receiver is debited a portion of that cost based on the tracing and weighting factors defined in the cycle allocation rules.

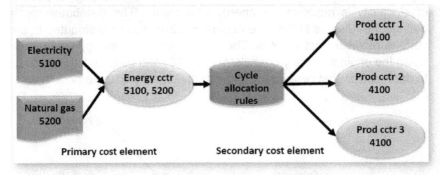

Figure 1.4: Assessment cycle

Like distribution cycles, assessment cycles can be used for both plan and actual postings, and they are easy to set up and maintain. The cycles are repeatable, but they have the same drawbacks as the distribution cycles regarding the accuracy of the allocations.

1.1.4 Indirect activity allocations

Indirect activity allocation cycles differ from distributions and assessments in that the outputs of the cycle are activity postings instead of cost element postings. The cycle calculates the quantity of activity that is posted to the sender for each receiver cost object. The cost that is allocated is the activity type price multiplied by the quantity of activity that was posted. The cost is credited to the sender and debited to the receiver using the secondary cost element assigned to the activity type. This method provides a much more sophisticated approach for determining the costs to be allocated than with distribution and assessment cycles. The amount allocated is based on the planned costs of the activity type and is not just dependent on a single cost element or grouping of cost elements; for example, the same cost element can be planned for multiple activity types in a cost center. Only that portion of the cost associated with the specific activity type is a part of the allocation.

Figure 1.5 shows how an indirect activity allocation cycle works. The cycle identifies a tracing factor associated with the receiver cost objects which is used in the calculation of activity quantities to be allocated from the sender cost object to various receivers. This tracing factor could be associated with postings by activity types, statistical key figures, or cost elements, among others. Based on this posting in each of the receivers, the cycle calculates the amount of activity to credit the sender cost center for each receiver object.

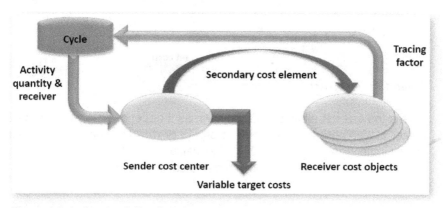

Figure 1.5: Indirect activity allocation cycle

These cycles are set up in a similar manner to the distribution and assessment cycles. Indirect activity allocations have some of the same drawbacks as the other types of cycles with regard to the lack of sophistication of the calculations. However, they can provide a higher level of accuracy than the others.

1.1.5 Target=Actual activity allocations

Target=Actual activity allocations are a special case of indirect activity allocation. This can only be used for actual postings. It uses receiver activity type posting as the tracing factor, and the weighting factor is based on the planned allocation of the sender activity for the receiver activity in the receiver cost centers.

Figure 1.6 shows that the indirect activity allocation uses the planned activity allocation from the sender as the tracing factor for each receiver. The allocation then works in the same way as the indirect activity allocation cycle.

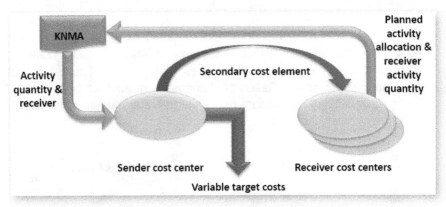

Figure 1.6: Target=Actual allocation

This is the easiest allocation to maintain as it depends solely on the cost center plan. There are no cycles to create or run, and they are handled by a single transaction (KNMA). The calculation of activity quantity is based on a specific case and this method cannot be used for planning.

1.1.6 Template allocations

Templates provide the most flexible and detailed method for generating cost allocations. Calculations can be defined based on various characteristics associated with the sender and receiver cost objects. The values of these characteristics can not only be used in the calculations, but can also be used to select different formulas, or even to determine which sender activity will be used.

Templates are assigned to environments. These provide access to sets of data fields associated with sender and receiver cost objects. Formulas are defined using the values of those data fields to calculate quantities of activity to allocate. The ability to create formulas using this data allows for much greater control in calculating the quantity of activity to allocate than any of the other methods that have been reviewed.

Figure 1.7 shows how a template allocation works. The template formulas calculate the activity quantity to post based on formulas which use data fields available to the specific environment for the allocation.

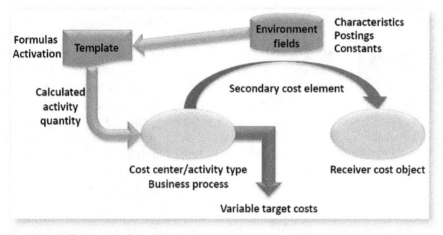

Figure 1.7: Template allocation

At first glance, creating and maintaining templates may seem daunting, but the rewards for using them can be great. Templates provide the most accurate means of allocating costs in CO, and once you understand the basics, you will find they are not so difficult to maintain and use.

1.2 Activity Based Costing

Templates were developed to support the Activity Based Costing module (CO-OM-ABC). The basis of Activity Based Costing is the definition of various activities within an organization and the assignment of costs to these activities. The activities are then assigned to products and services according to the actual consumption of these activities by each product and service. The activities are described by cost drivers, which combine both direct and indirect costs to identify a specific source of cost that occurs.

1.2.1 Cost drivers

A cost driver identifies the costs associated with a specific activity. Cost drivers can not only identify the cost of performing a specific activity, they can also represent the cost of not performing the activity. Manufacturing provides a good example.

Cost drivers in production

 Two different products run through the same production route within a plant. Product A runs at half the speed of product B. Running product B on the equipment causes more production stops that require shop personnel to come fix the issue. In addition, product B runs in smaller batch sizes, which requires additional setup and handling of the batches. We have identified three cost drivers in this example, each accounting for both direct and indirect costs. The first driver is machine run time, which at a minimum includes the cost of utilities and labor and may include other costs as well. Its unit of measure represents one hour of running the equipment. The driver cost for both products is the same, but the consumption of the driver is different for each one based on the speed. The second driver is the machine stop. While the machine is stopped, utilities are still consumed, and there is additional cost associated with the indirect labor and supplies required to get the machine restarted. The third driver is the batch change. This driver includes utilities associated with the stoppage of the equipment as well as requisite packaging material and labor required to process the batch change.

Traditional methods of allocating overhead cost to the products can easily account for the differences in machine speed, but the processing of stops and batch changes are a different matter. These costs tend to be smeared across all products without regard to individual product characteristics that affect the way the costs are actually being consumed. This could lead to erroneous understanding of the profitability of each product. Using standard allocation methods, it could appear that product A is more costly to produce than product B, due to its lower speed. However, due to the stop level and batch sizing considerations for B, product A could actually be the least costly alternative because the consumption of those drivers by B significantly drive up the cost of manufacturing.

The concept of the cost driver is not restricted to a manufacturing environment. In a customer service setting, drivers could include actions such as processing sales order line items or dealing with returns. The details provided by these drivers help give a better view of the total cost of operation.

1.2.2 Activity types and business processes

Activity types are simple forms of cost drivers. When planning costs on a cost center, certain costs can be associated with an activity type. This activity type is then used for allocation of those costs to another object, such as a product, production order, or even another cost center. The costs planned for an activity type in a cost center can include the costs that are directly planned in that cost center (direct costs) and also those that are allocated from another cost center or cost object (indirect costs). Machine run time is a good example of the use of an activity type. Manufacturing costs associated with running the machine are planned using an activity type in a cost center. Based on the connection of the cost center to a work center, an activity posting is made when production is confirmed at that work center. This consumes the calculated quantity of the machine run time activity.

More complex forms of drivers can be represented by other types of master data called *business processes*. A business process works in a similar fashion to a cost center/activity type combination. Costs are planned and allocated to business processes just as they are with cost center/activity types. Cost allocation from a business process uses a secondary cost element of type 43, just like activity types. What sets the business process apart is its independence from the cost center. This allows for a much clearer understanding of the values assigned to a cost driver than if that driver were represented by one of many activity types within a cost center. The cost performance of a driver represented by a business process also becomes much more visible.

The other two cost drivers in our example lend themselves to being represented by business processes. The costs are derived from multiple cost centers by allocation, and they describe specific repeatable functions. Using business processes to describe these drivers gives visibility of effectiveness in three areas. First, the number of occurrences of each driver reported affects the cost of the product and the manufacturing order. Second, the posting of these occurrences also impacts the originating overhead cost centers based on allocations and provides the necessary information to manage those cost centers. Finally, by allocating and posting actual costs to the business process, its performance can also be monitored to ensure that the proper costs have been assigned to it.

1.2.3   Templates and activity based costing

The simple calculations associated with traditional methods of cost allocation do not provide the necessary detail for costing with Activity Based Costing. SAP developed a better method of calculating activity quantities in order to take advantage of the cost granularity required. Templates provide access to master data characteristics and ABAP (Advanced Business Application Programming) functions which are used in calculations to determine driver quantities. In addition, templates use Boolean logic (true/false) to enable specific calculations under specific circumstances. This is what makes the template a powerful tool to use for accurately allocating costs. The sources of cost allocation in templates are the drivers defined by activity types and business processes.

1.3   Templates and how they work

The following example of cost allocations using a template provides a brief look into the workings of templates. Transaction CPT1 is used to create a template. The MAINT template is used to allocate maintenance costs from the plant maintenance cost center to a production cost center.

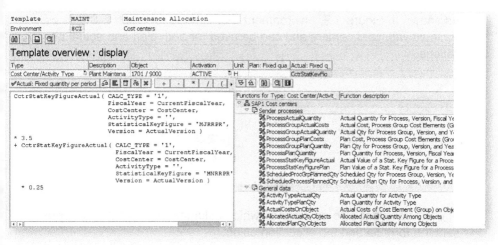

Figure 1.8: MAINT template

Figure 1.8 shows the MAINT template, which looks at postings in the production cost center of statistical key figures representing instances of different types of maintenance activity. In the image, MJRRPR represents a major repair, which consumes 3.5 hours of maintenance time. MNRRPR is a minor repair, which takes 15 minutes (0.25 hours) of maintenance time. Activity type 9000 (Maintenance) planned in cost center 1701 (Plant Maintenance) is used for the cost allocation.

1.3.1 Environments

The first thing to notice is that a template is assigned to a specific environment. The environment dictates how the template is used and what data is available to it. There are environments associated with Product Cost Controlling, Easy Cost Planning, and Cost Center Accounting, among others. Each environment has access to a set of data in specific tables for use in calculations. Functions specific to that environment are used to access that data and are also used in the formulas. The environment also determines which objects can be used for allocation and what types of allocations can be performed.

As shown in Figure 1.9, environment SCI is used for MAINT. SCI is associated with cost centers and can be used for both plan and actual allocations.

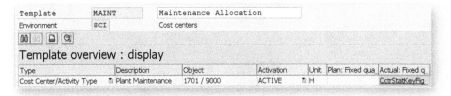

Figure 1.9: Environment and calculation row

The environment also determines which columns are available to represent the formula and the allocation object.

1.3.2 Calculation rows

The calculation row is the heart of the template. It is used to connect characteristics of the template environment with functions to form complex formulas which define allocation quantities. The SCI cost center environment has the following columns available for each calculation row:

▶ *Type* is the object type for the row. This usually identifies the method of allocation that is used, such as cost center/activity type or business process. Other object types will be reviewed in later chapters.

▶ *Description* is the description of the object used for allocation.

▶ *Object* identifies the cost object used for the allocation. In our example, this is cost center 1701/activity type 9000.

▶ *Activation* determines whether or not the calculation is to be executed for the allocation. A row can be ACTIVE or INACTIVE, and environment characteristics and functions can be used to specify if the row is active for this set of circumstances.

▶ *Unit* is the unit of measure of the allocation object.

▶ *Plan: Fixed quantity* contains the method used to calculate the allocation for plan costs.

▶ *Actual: Fixed quantity* contains the method used to calculate the allocation for actual costs.

Different environments have different columns available depending on the allocation needs in those environments. This will be discussed in further detail in later chapters.

The MAINT template allocates costs from cost center 1701 using activity type 9000 for each receiver that is assigned to this template. This calculation is always activated (*Activation* cell set to ACTIVE). Figure 1.10 shows the formula used to determine the allocation quantity. The current period posting for the statistical key figure MJRRPR comes from the receiving costing and multiplies that by the number of hours allocated to a major repair (3.5). It then adds to this the current period posting for the statistical key figure MNRRPR multiplied by 0.25.

```
✔Actual: Fixed quantity per period   🔀 📧 📋 👭 ✖    +   -   *   /   (  ▶

CctrStatKeyFigureActual( CALC_TYPE = '1',
                         FiscalYear = CurrentFiscalYear,
                         CostCenter = CostCenter,
                         ActivityType = '',
                         StatisticalKeyFigure = 'MJRRPR',
                         Version = ActualVersion )
* 3.5
+ CctrStatKeyFigureActual( CALC_TYPE = '1',
                           FiscalYear = CurrentFiscalYear,
                           CostCenter = CostCenter,
                           ActivityType = '',
                           StatisticalKeyFigure = 'MNRRPR'
                           Version = ActualVersion )
  * 0.25

◀ ▶                                              ◀ ▶
```

Figure 1.10: Formula used for calculating the activity allocation

`CctrStatKeyFigureActual` is a function that returns the quantity of a statistical key figure posted to the cost center specified in the function. In this case, `CostCenter` refers to the receiver cost center. The functions allow for access to specific data and characteristics in the environment and are central to what makes template allocations so powerful.

Functions for Type: Cost Center/Activit	Function description
▽ 品 SAP1 Cost centers	
▽ 🖵 Sender processes	
✇ ProcessActualQuantity	Actual Quantity for Process, Version, Fiscal Ye
✇ ProcessGroupActualCosts	Actual Cost, Process Group Cost Elements (Gr
✇ ProcessGroupActualQuantity	Actual Qty for Process Group, Version, and Ye
✇ ProcessGroupPlanCosts	Plan Cost, Process Group Cost Elements (Grou
✇ ProcessGroupPlanQuantity	Plan Qty for Process Group, Version, and Yea
✇ ProcessPlanQuantity	Plan Quantity for Process, Version, Fiscal Year
✇ ProcessStatKeyFigureActual	Actual Value of a Stat. Key Figure for a Proce：
✇ ProcessStatKeyFigurePlan	Plan Value of a Stat. Key Figure for a Process
✇ ScheduledProcGrpPlannedQty	Scheduled Qty for Process Group, Version, Ye
✇ ScheduledProcessPlannedQty	Scheduled Plan Qty for Process, Version, and
▽ 🖵 General data	
✇ ActivityTypeActualQty	Actual Quantity for Activity Type
✇ ActivityTypePlanQty	Plan Quantity for Activity Type
✇ ActualCostsOnObject	Actual Costs of Cost Element (Group) on Obje
✇ AllocatedActualQtyObjects	Allocated Actual Quantity Among Objects
✇ AllocatedPlanQtyObjects	Allocated Plan Quantity Among Objects
✇ CalculationRowResult	Use Result of Calculation Row
✇ CctrStatKeyFigureActual	Actual Value of a Stat. KF for CCtr/Activity Ty
✇ CostCtrStatKeyFigurePlan	Plan Value of a Stat. KF for CCtr/Activity Type

Figure 1.11: List of functions available in the environment

When defining the formula for calculating the quantity, the transaction provides a list of functions available for use in that column, as shown in Figure 1.11. Functions are used for determining row activation, object determination, or quantity formulas. Some functions can be useful for all three categories, but others can only be used for one or two of the categories. Functions that cannot be used for a specific column type are not displayed.

1.3.3 Connecting the template

After the template has been created and saved, it still needs to be assigned to a receiver object so that it can be invoked for allocation purposes. For template environment SCI, this is done by maintaining the master data of the receiver cost centers.

Run transaction KS02 for the receiver cost center and select the TEM-PLATES tab. Environment SCI is for activity-independent allocations and is assigned as shown in Figure 1.12. Only now can the allocation be performed.

Figure 1.12: Assigning the template to the receiver

This is the correct way to link templates to receivers in this environment. Other environments may require special configuration to define this assignment.

1.3.4 Executing the allocation

Our allocation requires that statistical key figures be posted in the receiving cost center. Figure 1.13 shows the postings for MJRRPR and MNRRPR in cost center 1301 that occurred in period 11.

CCtrs: Act./Tgt/Var.	Date:	12/11/2017
Cost center/group: 1301	Manufacturing Plant	
Person responsible: SAP		
Reporting period: 12 to 12 2017		

Statistical key figures	Actual	P.
MJRRPR Major Repair	20 EA	
MNRRPR Minor Repair	157 EA	

Figure 1.13: Statistical key figure postings in cost center 1301

Transaction KPAS is used to perform the actual template allocation for cost centers. After executing the transaction, the posting is made using cost center 1701/activity type 9000 with cost center 1301 as the receiver, as shown in Figure 1.14.

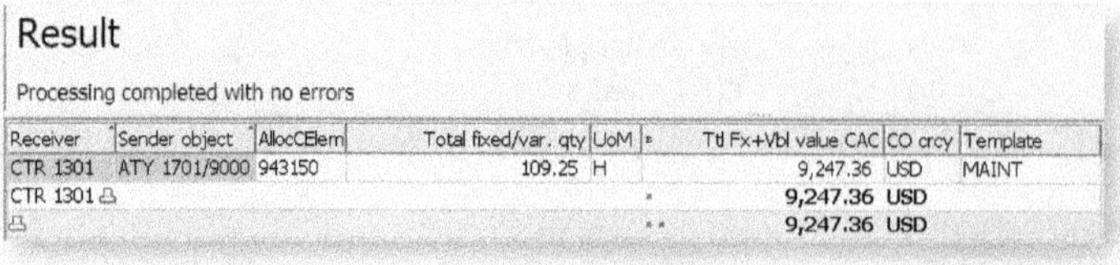

Result

Processing completed with no errors

Receiver	Sender object	AllocCElem	Total fixed/var. qty	UoM	*	Ttl Fx+Vbl value CAC	CO crcy	Template
CTR 1301	ATY 1701/9000	943150	109.25	H		9,247.36	USD	MAINT
CTR 1301					*	9,247.36	USD	
					**	9,247.36	USD	

Figure 1.14: Results of the template allocation

According to the template, the number of postings of MJRRPR should be multiplied by 3.5 to give the quantity of activity type 9000 associated with that statistical key figure (20 multiplied by 3.5 gives 70). Similarly, the occurrences of MNRRPR should be multiplied by 0.25 to calculate the quantity of activity type 9000 associated with it (157 multiplied by 0.25 gives 39.25). Adding these two together results in a total activity quantity of 109.25 hours, which is what was posted to cost center 1701, with allocation to receiver cost center 1301.

2 Templates in product costing

Templates are made up of rows and columns that are used to calculate allocation quantities. Each row of a template defines an allocation for cost objects using calculations and characteristics assigned to the columns. Product cost estimates can use templates to generate detailed cost allocations from cost centers and business processes that are much more specific than other standard allocation techniques. In looking at how product cost estimates use templates, we are introduced to the concepts of how rows and columns work together to generate the allocations.

2.1 Costing scenario

Chapter 1 introduced a process for using templates to allocate activities to a cost center. The standard way for assigning activity costs in product costing is through the costing definition of work centers that are used in a routing. Cost center/activity type costs are allocated to the product using the formulas assigned to the work center based on the lot size quantity assigned to the material cost estimate. This works well for picking up machine and labor costs, but other overhead costs cannot be determined in detail without using templates. They can calculate activity quantities that are based on specific characteristics associated with the material and the order. The following product costing scenario further demonstrates the power of templates and template allocations.

Plant P100 makes widgets. At the beginning of each production order, the production support department spends two hours setting up the machine. After every 100 widgets are made, the production support department needs to recalibrate the machine. This takes 30 minutes. A finished widget is packed at the end of the process. Packaging requirements vary based on the weight of the widget and whether the widget is declared as a dangerous good. A maximum of 250 kg can be loaded onto a pallet. If a widget is declared a dangerous good, then a special pallet is required for shipping purposes. This special pallet is not only more expensive than standard pallets, but also requires extra handling costs. Quality inspection is performed for each widget. This requires looking at each individual component as well as the final product, and takes half a minute per material. Any widget components that are considered dangerous goods require additional inspection. This inspection takes 1 minute per component.

Three cost centers are used when manufacturing widgets. Cost center 1301 is the manufacturing cost center and the work center WMAKER (Widget Maker) is assigned to that cost center. There are two activity types used for picking up overhead costs from 1301. These are 1000 (machine hours), and 2000 (labor hours). Cost center 1501 is the manufacturing support cost center. This cost center is responsible for machine setups and calibrations. Activity type 9010 represents the cost of 1 hour of services from this cost center. Cost center 1601 is the quality control cost center and is responsible for inspection of the widget components. Activity type 9020 represents the cost of 1 hour of inspection time. Two packaging business processes are used to represent the cost of palletizing and shipping the widgets. Plan costs include both the cost of the pallet and the labor and supply cost associated with preparing the widgets for shipment. Business process BP001 is associated with standard pallets. Business process BP002 represents special pallets that are required when handling dangerous goods.

The material cost estimate for the widgets should not only include the cost of the components, but also the costs of manufacturing, machine setup, quality inspections, and shipping. The manufacturing cost is determined from the formulas and activity types assigned to the WMAKER work center. The remaining costs are determined by using the MANU-FACT template.

2.2 Cost estimate

Material A-100 is a widget that has two components. One B-100 and one B-101 are assembled to make one A-100 unit. The net weight of the final product is 4.1 kg, which is defined on the BASIC 1 tab of the material master, as shown in Figure 2.1.

Dimensions/EANs			
Gross Weight	4.100	Weight Unit	KG
Net Weight	4.100		

Figure 2.1: A-100 weights

The dangerous goods profile is defined on the BASIC 2 tab (see Figure 2.2). Here, it is blank, which indicates that this material is not classified as a dangerous good.

Environment	
DG indicator profile	

Figure 2.2: A-100 dangerous goods profile

The costing lot size as defined on the COSTING 1 tab is 1,000 and the overhead group assignment is WIDGET (see Figure 2.3). Overhead key WIDGET is assigned to that overhead group.

Origin group		Material origin	
Overhead Group	WIDGET	Variance Key	000001
Plant-sp.matl status			
Valid from		Profit Center	
Quantity structure data			
Alternative BOM		BOM Usage	
Group		Group Counter	
Task List Type			
SpecProcurem Costing		Costing Lot Size	1,000

Figure 2.3: A-100 overhead group and costing lot size

A template MANUFACT has been defined to account for the special costing scenarios, as defined in Section 2.1. A cost estimate has been created for material A-100 in plant P100.

| | Costing Data | Dates | Qty Struct. | Valuation | History | Costs |

Costs Based On   Costing Lot Size   1,000

Itemization for material A-100 in plant P100

ItmNo	I	Resource			Cost Element	¤	Total Value	Currncy	Quantity	Un
1	E	1301	WMAKER	1000	943001		10,000.00	USD	50.00	H
2	E	1301	WMAKER	2000	943002		3,500.00	USD	100.00	H
3	M	P100 B-100			400000		5,000.00	USD	1,000	EA
4	M	P100 B-101			400000		9,000.00	USD	1,000	EA
5	E	1501		9010	943160		337.50	USD	4.50	H
6	E	1501		9010	943160		150.00	USD	2.00	H
7	E	1601		9020	943170		750.02	USD	16.667	H
8	X	BP001			943100		170.00	USD	17	EA
							▪ 28,907.52	USD		

Figure 2.4: A-100 cost estimate

The cost estimate itemization is shown in Figure 2.4 and is explained below:

❶ Items 1–4 on the itemization are the costs associated with the route and the bill of material (BOM).

❷ Item 5 on the cost estimate is the recalibration cost using activity type 9010 from the cost center manufacturing support cost center 1501. After the first 100 items are produced, recalibration should begin. Because the costing size is 1,000, there should be 9 recalibration activities, each taking 30 minutes. This results in 4.5 hours of recalibration work for 1,000 widgets.

❸ Item 6 is the initial machine setup for the run of 1,000 widgets. This process takes 2 hours. The same cost center and activity type is used for the fixed setup time and for the recalibration.

❹ Item 7 is the inspection time. The activity type is from the quality control cost center. Because this is not considered a dangerous good, the component inspection only takes 30 seconds per material. There are 2 components in the BOM and this accounts for 1 minute of inspection for each widget. The activity time is therefore 1,000 minutes, which equates to 16.667 hours.

❺ Item 8 is the packaging cost. The dangerous goods profile is blank, so the standard pallet business process (BP001) is used in the cost estimate. This business process accounts for both the cost of the pallet and the processing that is required for preparing the pallet for shipment. The net weight of the material is 4.1 kg. The total number of widgets that can be assigned to a pallet is 60.98 (250/4.1). A partial widget does not make sense, and so the most number of widgets that can be put on a pallet is 60. Therefore, the quantity of pallets required for 1,000 widgets is 16.667 (1,000/60). However, since a fraction of a pallet cannot be used, 16.667 is rounded up to 17.

2.3   Connecting the template to the cost estimate

The result of the cost estimate in Section 2.2 matched the specifications for packaging, setup, recalibration, and testing. This was all accomplished by using the MANUFACT template. Section 1.3.3 discussed how templates need to be connected to the receiver objects so that their calculations can be used. In the case of cost centers, this is done by assigning the template directly to the applicable cost centers through master data maintenance. A more flexible approach has been developed for dealing with objects where the master data is less permanent, such as for orders or material cost estimates. Overhead costing sheets were already set up to use overhead keys assigned to the material master in order for them to be accessed for product costing. This same strategy was adapted for use with template allocations. The use of an overhead key is much more generic than directly assigning a template to the material and can point to different overhead structures depending on plant and costing variants.

Costing sheets are accessible to cost estimates through the valuation variant assigned to the costing variant of the cost estimate. The costing sheet is assigned to the valuation variant of the cost estimate; this is covered in Section 4.5. Because this connection already existed, assigning the template to a specific costing sheet also enables it to be accessed by the cost estimate. Section 4.4 provides details of the configuration using transaction KTPF through the use of overhead keys. Different overhead keys can be set up to connect to different templates, making it possible to use different sets of calculations depending on the material being costed.

When a cost estimate is created, the costing sheet is connected to it based on the valuation variant configuration. The overhead key is used for two reasons. First, it determines which overhead calculations are used by the costing sheet. Using transactions KK11 and KK12, the overhead key can be assigned values for the overhead conditions defined in the costing sheet to add the appropriate overhead costs. If the overhead key is not assigned to one of the overhead conditions, the calculations are bypassed. The second use for the overhead key is to specify the connection to a template. In this case, the connection is based on configuration associating the costing sheet, the overhead key, and the template. The VALUATION tab of the cost estimate shows this association for the material. In this scenario, the overhead key WIDGET is not assigned to any overhead costing sheet conditions, so only the allocations associated with the template are included in the cost estimate.

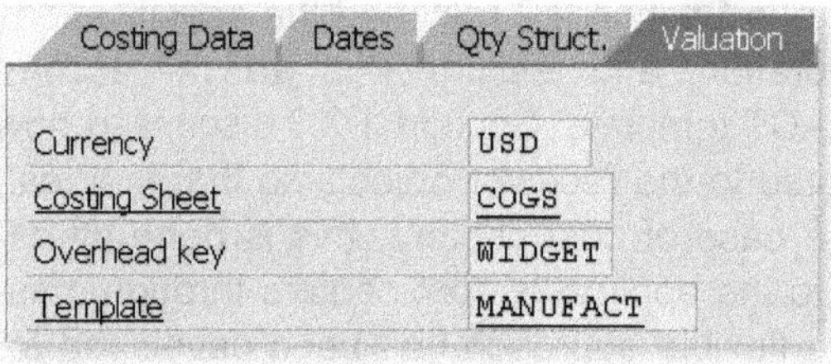

Costing Data	Dates	Qty Struct.	Valuation
Currency		USD	
Costing Sheet		COGS	
Overhead key		WIDGET	
Template		MANUFACT	

Figure 2.5: A-100 cost estimate valuation tab

The VALUATION tab for this cost estimate (see Figure 2.5) shows that the overhead key WIDGET was used to connect template MANUFACT for the special calculations required.

2.4 Template maintenance

Transactions CPT1, CPT2, CPT3, and CPT4 are used for maintaining templates. CPT1 is for creation, CPT2 is for modification, CPT3 is for display, and CPT4 is for deletion. Template data is considered configuration, and when saving a template, the system requests a transport be assigned to the changes.

Creating a template

The MANUFACT template was created using transaction CPT1 (see Figure 2.6).

Figure 2.6: Creating a template

Select a template ID and assign it to an environment. When creating a new template, an existing template can be copied by entering its information in the Reference area of the initial CPT1 window. After pressing Enter , the maintenance view is displayed (see Figure 2.7).

Template IDs and environments

The same template ID can be used in multiple environments. For example, a MANUFACT template could be used in environment 001 (production orders) and also in environment 009 (process orders). The sets of sub-environments and functions available for creating the allocation rows are different for environment 009 and environment 001. The connection of a template to an allocation is environment-specific and a template defined for environment 001 cannot be used in an application that requires environment 009. It can be convenient to use the same ID for templates with similar uses in different environments.

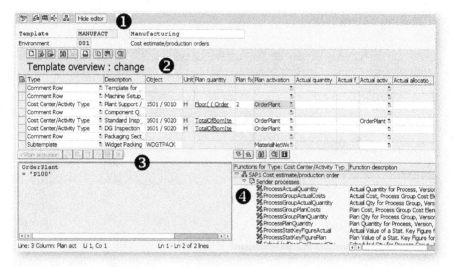

Figure 2.7: Template maintenance view

There are four sections in the maintenance window:

❶ The top section asks for a descriptive name for the template.

❷ The template structure is defined in this section. The columns associated with the environment are displayed by default, and rows of various types can be added, modified, or deleted at this point. A full description of this process is covered in Section 2.6.

❸ The editor section is used for creating and modifying formulas and methods that are used for object determination, row activation, quantity calculations, and allocation events. The procedures for this are covered in Chapter 3.

❹ This section contains a list of all template functions that are applicable to the specific row and column that is being edited. These functions are maintained using transaction CTU6, and this is covered in Chapter 4.

Modifying a template

Templates can be modified using transaction CPT2. This is also useful for regenerating templates that have been changed and transported to another client. Execute CPT2, select the template and environment, and then click on the ⊕ button to make sure that all the latest changes have been made active. If you don't do this, the older version of the template might still be useable, which could cause improper calculations to occur. Two other buttons are available: the ⬛ button displays the hierarchy of templates and shows all templates that have been defined and where subtemplates are assigned, and the ⇨ button shows the structures to which the selected template is assigned.

Displaying a template

Transaction CPT3 displays the selected template. Once in the maintenance screen, clicking on the 🐦 button returns to the initial window, but the transaction is changed to CPT2. Press ⎡Enter⎤ to return to the template details.

Deleting a template

Template deletion is performed using transaction CPT4. Enter the template and environment and press ⎡Enter⎤. If the template is not assigned directly to a cost object or used as a subtemplate, a small window is displayed to confirm the deletion, as shown in Figure 2.8.

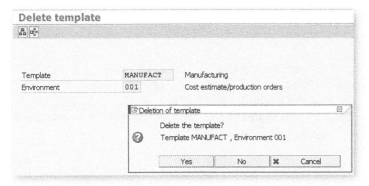

Figure 2.8: Delete template using CPT4

Care must be taken when deleting templates that are used for product costing as they are not directly assigned to a cost object. Make sure that the template is not still in use.

2.5 Template columns

Templates are similar to spreadsheets in that they have rows and columns for calculations. However, the rows and columns of a template are not as generic as those of a spreadsheet, and they have specific meanings and purposes. Different environments use different row and column types that are suited to the purpose of each environment. Each column represents a specific function within the environment. A column can identify the sender for the allocation, whether a row is active and used in the calculation, or an allocation quantity calculation.

> ### Columns, rows, and cells
>
> Each template *column* represents a specific function. The column can be used for object determination, a specific type of quantity calculation, or for other purposes. For each row in the template, the column has exactly the same function. The template *row* defines a specific action to be taken by the template. Rows can be used for quantity calculations and allocations, special reusable formulas, or for invoking a subtemplate, and other actions. A *cell* is the intersection of a row and a column. The cell contains the specific instructions for how the column is to be used for that specific row.

Environment 001 for cost estimates and production orders is a part of the COB (cost object) template application. All environments (001 - 012) associated with this application have the same column structure. The following sections identify the columns used by the COB template application and their uses in the template calculations.

2.5.1 Type column

The TYPE column identifies the use of a specific row. A row can be used for allocation quantity calculations, subtemplate execution, reusable calculations, or for comments to document the actions of the template. Depending on which object type is selected for a row, certain columns will be disabled for that row. For a description of how each row type is used, refer to Section 2.6.

2.5.2   Description column

The DESCRIPTION field is used to enter a 30-character description of the row. For certain row types, the description may default to the ID of the assigned object. This can be overridden to provide a more detailed description of the row's purpose.

2.5.3   Object column

The OBJECT column contains the object associated with the row. This could be an allocation object, a reusable calculation ID, a subtemplate, or one of several other types, depending on the environment.

If the row is an allocation type, the object defines one or more allocation sender objects. A business process row requires that the object returned be a business process or a set of business processes. A cost center/activity type row expects the object to be a cost center/activity type combination. Allocation objects can be explicitly defined or derived using functions. The function can return either a single object or a set of objects. If returning a set of objects, the allocation for the row applies to every object in the set.

Calculation rows contain reusable formulas used for quantity determinations. The object column contains the ID for the formula that can be referenced in other rows of the template. The use of calculation rows is described in detail in Chapter 3.

The object column in a subtemplate row contains a template ID. This template is an extension of the current template, and when active, it is processed as if it were a part of the main template. The subtemplate must be created in the same environment as the main template.

2.5.4   Unit column

The UNIT column is not enabled for editing. This shows the unit of measure defined for the object used for allocation. Templates for Easy Cost Planning enable the unit of measure to be defined in the object determination for V item (variable) cost rows.

2.5.5   Quantity columns

The QUANTITY column contains the formulas that are used to calculate the quantities for allocation rows or for reusable calculation rows. There can be several different quantity columns in a single row: four are defined for environments of the COB application, two are used for plan allocations (variable and fixed), and two are used for actual allocations (variable and fixed). The formula used for quantity determination could consist of a single constant value or could be a more complex calculation using a mixture of constants, template functions, and arithmetic operators. The goal is to calculate an allocation quantity based on the data available to the environment.

2.5.6   Activation columns

The ACTIVATION column is used to determine whether the formula or action described for the row will be active when the template is invoked. The value returned is "true" if the row is processed, or "false" if the row should be bypassed. The process used for determining this involves a combination of template functions, constant values, and logical operators. COB application templates have two activation columns. One is for plan allocations and the other is for actual allocations. Actual allocations may be triggered by different criteria than for plan allocations. For this reason, there are separate activations for each type of allocation.

2.5.7   Allocation event columns

The ALLOCATION EVENT column is a special column used for cost object (COB) application environments. If left blank, this column has no impact on the allocation. If an event is found, the function called returns a period number during which the event occurred. If the event hasn't happened, the function returns a 0 and no quantity is allocated. Only if the event is defined and the period returned matches the allocation period is the calculation performed. Usually, allocation events are only used for actual allocations. However, templates for work breakdown structure (WBS) elements and networks also allow for plan allocation events. Allocation events normally refer to status change dates in orders, and trigger allocations based on the status change. Many of the objects that use allocation events refer to orders. Orders are not fiscal period dependent, but cost allocations that depend on order status should only be performed when that status is set and not for each fiscal period that the order is active.

2.5.8   Effect of environment on columns

The columns which are available to each environment are defined by SAP. Different applications have different requirements for allocations, thereby affecting which columns are available for use. Only the COB application has a use for allocation events, for example. Other environments might only calculate plan values and have no need for formulas working on actual data. Easy Cost Planning even has an additional PRICE column, which is used for assigning a unit cost for items with category V (variable). When creating a template for a specific environment, make sure to understand which columns are available and what place they have in the calculations.

2.6   Template rows

The rows are the mathematical engine of the template. They contain the formulas that are used for calculating the allocations when the template is executed. When a new template is created, several empty rows are made available. When working on any new row, first select the row type. This is done by using the dropdown menu in the TYPE cell for that row, as shown in Figure 2.9.

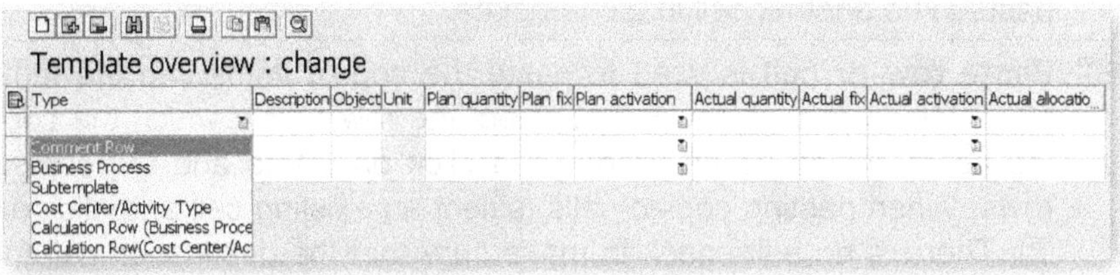

Figure 2.9: Selecting the row type

Once the row type is selected, only cells in the columns allowed for that row type are available for editing. The other cells are "grayed out", preventing their use. The appropriate information can then be added to the row, and processing continues with the next available row. When there are no more rows left, the edit buttons at the top of the section can be used to create more empty rows, copy existing rows, or for other general editing functions. These buttons are:

□ **Append** is used to create a new row at the bottom of the template structure.

▣ **Insert** is used to create a new row immediately before the selected row. Select the row by clicking in the selection box immediately to the left of the TYPE column. Next, click on ▣ and an empty row is displayed above to the selected row. It is also possible to insert multiple rows by selecting 2 or more existing rows. There are two ways that rows can be selected, which affect how the rows are inserted. Rows that are selected using the ⌂ -mouse click method are all adjacent, and new rows are added above to the first row selected. The number of rows added is the same as the number of rows selected. If the Ctrl -mouse click method is used, the individual selections are treated separately, and one new row is added prior to each selected row, even if the selected rows are adjacent.

▣ **Delete** is used to remove a row from the template. Select the row or rows to be deleted and click on the button. Those rows are then deleted from the template.

▣ **Copy row or cell** serves two purposes. It can be used to copy a row, or multiple rows, to be appended to another section of the template. To do this, select the row(s) to be copied and click on the ▣ button. The rows are then kept in a paste buffer for later insertion into the template. This can also be used to copy a single cell. Click in the cell and click on the ▣ button. The copied cell can then be pasted into another cell in the template.

▣ **Paste row or cell** is used to paste the copied items into the template. When pasting rows, first select the row above which the copied items should be inserted. Then click on ▣ to add the copied rows. When pasting copied cells, select an existing cell and click on ▣.There is no edit check to make sure that the destination cell for the paste action is compatible with the contents of the original cell. The contents of the destination cell could be invalid.

▣ **Print** sends the template information to the printer.

⊞ **Search** brings up a dialog box into which a search string can be entered. The focus changes to the first cell in which the string is found.

⊞ **Search next** is only enabled once an initial search has been performed. It sets the focus to the cell containing the next occurrence of the string.

⊞ **Edit cell** is used to switch to the editor section of the screen for the cell that is selected. This can also be accomplished by double clicking in the cell. This is covered in detail in Chapter 3.

2.6.1 Business process row

The business process row is a quantity allocation type row. The object determination column for this row type must point to a business process or a group of business processes. Plan and actual allocations can be made for this row type. A specific business process can be selected, or functions can be used to derive a business process or a set of business processes. If a set of business processes is returned, any quantity that is calculated for the allocation applies to all the business processes returned.

As shown in Figure 2.10, a business process can be explicitly assigned in the OBJECT column. The system converts this into a function call such as SenderProcess = 'BP001'. Section 3.3.4 explains how to set up the object determination cell.

Template overview : display

Type	Description	Object	Unit	Plan quantity	Plan fix	Plan activation	Actual quantity	Actual f	Actual activation	Actual allocatio
Business Process	Standard Pallets	BP001	EA	Cell OrderTotal		MaterialNetWei			≈	
Business Process	DG Pallets	BP002	EA	Cell OrderTotal		MaterialNetWei			≈	

Figure 2.10: Business process row

2.6.2 Cost center/activity type row

The allocation object for this row type is a cost center/activity type combination. Although the allocation object is different, the definition of the row and how it works is the same as for business processes. The object returned in the OBJECT column must be a cost center/activity type or a group of cost center/activity type pairings. A specific cost center and activity type can be assigned (see Figure 2.11) and this is also converted into functions in the OBJECT cell, similar to the following: `SenderCostCenter = '1601' AND SenderActivityType = '9020'`.

	Type	Description	Object	Unit	Plan quantity	Plan fix	Plan activation	Actual quantity	Actual fix	Actual activation	Actual allocatio
	Cost Center/Activity Type	Standard Insp	1601 / 9020	H	TotalOfBomIte		OrderPlant			OrderPlant	
	Cost Center/Activity Type	DG Inspection	1601 / 9020	H	TotalOfBomIte		OrderPlant				

Template overview : change

Figure 2.11: Cost center/activity type row

2.6.3 Calculation row

The calculation row is used to create a common formula that can be used as part of the formula in other rows of the template. This alleviates the need for recreating a calculation in multiple formulas in the template. A name is assigned to the calculation row so that it can be referenced in other formulas. This name is defined in the Object column (see Figure 2.12). Calculation row formulas can be used in each of the available formula columns.

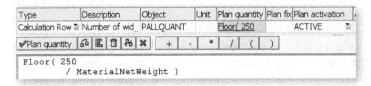

Type	Description	Object	Unit	Plan quantity	Plan fix	Plan activation	
Calculation Row	Number of wid	PALLQUANT		Floor(250		ACTIVE	

✔Plan quantity `+ - * / ( )`

```
Floor( 250
        / MaterialNetWeight )
```

Figure 2.12: Calculation row

Two template functions can be used to reference calculation rows in other formulas: `CalculationRowResult` is used to return the value of a formula within the current template, and `ResultOfGlobalCalcRow` returns the value of a formula from another accessible template.

Type	Description	Object	Unit	Plan quantity	Plan fix	Plan activation	
Business Process	Standard Pallets	BP001	EA	Ceil(OrderTotal		MaterialNetWe	

✔Plan quantity `+ - * / ( )`

```
Ceil( OrderTotalQuantity
        / CalculationRowResult( CalculationRowName = 'PALLQUANT'
                                Column = CurrentColumn ) )
```

Figure 2.13: Using a calculation row in a formula

Figure 2.13 shows how a calculation row is accessed in another formula. The result is considered to be just another operand in the current formula. Row ID and column are required in the function to identify which formula should be used.

The COB application environments, of which 001 is a member, support two different types of calculation rows. There is one specifically defined for use in business process rows and another one for cost center/activity type rows. The different calculation rows have access to different functions based on the intended use in allocation formulas. The cost center/activity type calculation row uses sender activity type functions, and the business process calculation row uses sender business process functions. This distinction is important when using the calculation row for allocation formulas to ensure that the proper type of reusable formula is being called upon in an allocation type row.

2.6.4   Subtemplate row

The subtemplate rows are used to access other templates in the environment. Templates can become very complex to view and maintain. Subtemplates provide an excellent way of breaking down the complexity and simplifying maintenance. A subtemplate is invoked from a main template from the subtemplate row, as seen in Figure 2.14.

Type	Description	Object	Unit	Plan quantity	Plan fix	Plan activation
Subtemplate	Widget Packing	WDGTPACK				MaterialNetWe

Figure 2.14: Subtemplate row

The object defined is the name of the template with the description defaulting to the template name. The only other columns enabled for subtemplate rows are the plan and actual activation columns. Like other row objects, subtemplates can be called up based on certain conditions defined in the activation column. If activated, the rows of the subtemplate are processed as if they were an integral part of the main template. The rows for subtemplate WDGTPACK in Figure 2.15 are processed if the row in Figure 2.14 is activated.

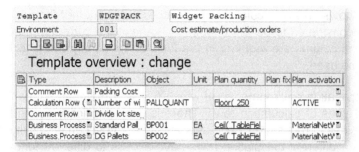

Figure 2.15: Subtemplate called up from the subtemplate row

Another benefit of using subtemplates is that they do not have to be directly assigned to a receiver object. Only the main template requires that connection.

2.6.5 Comment row

Comment rows are available in all environments. The sole purpose is to create a place to document what is happening in the template. Comment rows make it easier to understand how the template is used and to identify blocks of rows that logically fit together. Comment rows are never active and are used for documentation purposes only.

Figure 2.16: Comment row

Select the "Comment Row" type and enter the description (see Figure 2.16). The description can be 30 characters long. If the description requires more characters, additional comment rows should be inserted.

2.6.6 Effect of environment on rows

The rows that are available for use vary by application. All environments within an application use the same row types. Many row types are common to multiple applications, but depending on the application, certain row types do not make sense. For example, the account type rows for application PCA (Profit Center Planning) aren't usable when dealing with cost objects of application COB, such as orders and cost estimates. Table 7.5 provides a list of rows by application. Easy Cost Planning (ECP) uses the greatest variety of row types. This is covered in detail in Chapter 6.

2.7 Cost estimate revisited

Now that the template structures have been explained, the cost estimate from Section 2.2 will be reviewed to tie the results back to the MANU-FACT template. Figure 2.17 shows the cost estimate for material A-100.

Costing Data	Dates	Qty Struct.	Valuation	History	Costs

| Costs Based On | | Costing Lot Size | | 1,000 | |

Itemization for material A-100 in plant P100

	ItmNo	I	Resource			Cost Element	≡	Total Value	Currncy	Quantity	Un
	1	E	1301	WMAKER	1000	943001		10,000.00	USD	50.00	H
❶	2	E	1301	WMAKER	2000	943002		3,500.00	USD	100.00	H
	3	M	P100 B-100			400000		5,000.00	USD	1,000	EA
	4	M	P100 B-101			400000		9,000.00	USD	1,000	EA
❷	5	E	1501		9010	943160		337.50	USD	4.50	H
❸	6	E	1501		9010	943160		150.00	USD	2.00	H
❹	7	E	1601		9020	943170		750.02	USD	16.667	H
❺	8	X	BP001			943100		170.00	USD	17	EA
							▪	28,907.52	USD		

Figure 2.17: A-100 cost estimate revisited

The cost estimate from Section 2.2 uses the following data from the material master and BOM:

► net weight: 4.1 kg (BASIC 1 tab of material master)

► dangerous goods profile: blank (BASIC 2 tab of material master)

► overhead group and key: WIDGET (COSTING 1 tab of material master)

► costing lot size: 1,000 (COSTING 1 tab of material master)

► number of BOM items: 2 (Bill of material maintenance)

The template that is used in the cost estimate is MANUFACT, which was selected based on the WIDGET overhead key. The template in Figure

2.18 starts with a section for machine setup and recalibration. There is one allocation row for cost center/activity types that contains formulas for both variable (recalibration) and fixed (setup) allocations. The next section of the template is for quality inspection. Here, there are two cost center/activity type allocation rows. One is for standard inspection and the other is for dangerous goods inspection. The final section of the template is for packaging. A subtemplate is executed to handle the allocation of pallets to the cost.

Template	MANUFACT	Manufacturing					
Environment	001	Cost estimate/production orders					

Template overview : change

Type	Description	Object	Unit	Plan quantity	Plan fix	Plan activation
Comment Row	Template for ...					
Comment Row	Machine Setup ...					
Cost Center/Activity Type	Plant Support / ...	1501 / 9010	H	Floor((Order ...	2	OrderPlant
Comment Row	Component Q ...					
Cost Center/Activity Type	Standard Insp ...	1601 / 9020	H	TotalOfBomIte ...		OrderPlant
Cost Center/Activity Type	DG Inspection	1601 / 9020	H	TotalOfBomIte ...		OrderPlant
Comment Row	Packaging Sect ...					
Subtemplate	Widget Packing	WDGTPACK				MaterialNetWe ...

Figure 2.18: MANUFACT template

The subtemplate WDGTPACK is shown in Figure 2.19. It contains a calculation row (PALLQUANT) and two business process allocation rows.

Template	WDGTPACK	Widget Packing				
Environment	001	Cost estimate/production orders				

Template overview : display

Type	Description	Object	Unit	Plan quantity	Plan fix	Plan activation
Comment Row	Packing Cost f ...					
Calculation Row (B	Number of wid ...	PALLQUANT		Floor(250		ACTIVE
Comment Row	Divide lot size ...					
Business Process	Standard Pallets	BP001	EA	Ceil(OrderTotal		MaterialNetWe ...
Business Process	DG Pallets	BP002	EA	Ceil(OrderTotal ...		MaterialNetWe ...

Figure 2.19: WDGTPACK subtemplate

2.7.1   A-100 recalibration cost

Item 5 of the cost estimate (❷) represents the recalibration costs. 4.5 hours of activity have been allocated to the cost estimate for recalibration. First, the activation status of the allocation row is checked (see Figure 2.20).

Type	Description	Object	Unit	Plan quantity	Plan fix	Plan activation	
Cost Center/Activity Type	Plant Support /	1501 / 9010	H	Floor((Order	2	OrderPlant	
Comment Row	Component Q						
Cost Center/Activity Type	Standard Insp	1601 / 9020	H	TotalOfBomIte		OrderPlant	
Cost Center/Activity Type	DG Inspection	1601 / 9020	H	TotalOfBomIte		OrderPlant	
Comment Row	Packaging Sect						

✔Plan activation   🔠 E 🗑 🖧 🖼 ✖   AND | OR | IN | = | <>   ▸   ▽ ◬ 🔱 ◎ 🏳

```
OrderPlant
= 'P100'
```
Functions for Type: C
▽ 🔠 SAP1 Cost estim

Figure 2.20: Setup/recalibration allocation activation

The `OrderPlant` function in the activation method returns the value of the plant selected in the cost estimate. This is compared with the string 'P100' and, since the material belongs to P100, the row is activated. Recalibration is the variable portion for allocating the costs from the production support cost center. The variable formula is shown in Figure 2.21.

Type	Description	Object	Unit	Plan quantity	Plan fix	Plan activation	
Cost Center/Activity Type	Plant Support /	1501 / 9010	H	Floor((Order	2	OrderPlant	
Comment Row	Component Q						
Cost Center/Activity Type	Standard Insp	1601 / 9020	H	TotalOfBomIte		OrderPlant	
Cost Center/Activity Type	DG Inspection	1601 / 9020	H	TotalOfBomIte		OrderPlant	
Comment Row	Packaging Sect						

✔Plan quantity   🔠 E 🗑 🖧 ✖   + | - | * | / | (|)   ▽ ◬ 🔱 ◎ ▣

```
Floor( ( OrderTotalQuantity
        - 100
      )
        / 100 )
* 0.5
```
Functions for Type: C
▽ 🔠 SAP1 Cost estim
  ▽ 🗔 Sender proce
    ℀ ProcessAc
    ℀ ProcessGr
    ℀ ProcessGr

Figure 2.21: Recalibration formula

Because recalibration only starts after 100 EA (eaches) have been produced, this formula takes the costing lot size (`OrderTotalQuantity` function) and subtracts 100 from it. This gives a value of 900. This is then divided by 100 and rounded down to the nearest whole number

(Floor function). This gives a value of 9. This result is multiplied by 0.5 (30 minutes or half an hour) which gives a value of 4.5 hours to allocate.

Type	Description	Object	Unit	Plan quantity	Plan fix	Plan activation	
Cost Center/Activity Type	⬚ Plant Support /	1501 / 9010	H	Floor((Order	2	OrderPlant	⬚
Comment Row	⬚ Component Q						⬚
Cost Center/Activity Type	⬚ Standard Insp	1601 / 9020	H	TotalOfBomIte		OrderPlant	⬚
Cost Center/Activity Type	⬚ DG Inspection	1601 / 9020	H	TotalOfBomIte		OrderPlant	⬚
Comment Row	⬚ Packaging Sect						⬚

| ✔Object | 🔁 | 🖹 | 🗑 | 🖇 | 🗗 | ✖ | | AND | IN | = | <> | < | > | <, | ⬇ | ⬆ | 🅗 | 🔍 | ▽ |

SenderCostCenter = '1501' AND	Functions for Type: C
SenderActivityType = '9010'	▽ 🔁 SAP1 Cost estim
	▽ 🖵 Order data

Figure 2.22: Recalibration allocation object

The allocation type is cost center/activity type. The specific object is defined in the Object column. The cost center and activity type were explicitly assigned using the object determination method, as shown in Figure 2.22.

2.7.2   A-100 setup cost

Item 6 of the cost estimate (❸) is the setup cost. This uses the same cost center/activity type as the recalibration cost (❷) from the cost estimate). The allocation for this is fixed and only occurs once for the quantity represented by the costing lot size. It remains the same for any costing lot size. If the row is activated, both the variable and fixed formulas are used for allocation.

Type	Description	Object	Unit	Plan quantity	Plan fix	Plan activation	
Cost Center/Activity Type	⬚ Plant Support /	1501 / 9010	H	Floor((Order	2	OrderPlant	⬚
Comment Row	⬚ Component Q						
Cost Center/Activity Type	⬚ Standard Insp	1601 / 9020	H	TotalOfBomIte		OrderPlant	⬚
Cost Center/Activity Type	⬚ DG Inspection	1601 / 9020	H	TotalOfBomIte		OrderPlant	⬚
Comment Row	⬚ Packaging Sect						⬚

| ✔Plan fix | 🔁 | 🖹 | 🗑 | 🖇 | ✖ | | + | - | * | / | (|) | | ⬇ | ⬆ | 🅗 | 🔍 | 🔲 |

2	Functions for Type: C
	▽ 🖳 SAP1 Cost estim

Figure 2.23: Setup formula

The formula in Figure 2.23 is very simple. It returns the value of a numeric constant. Therefore, 2 hours of the activity are "calculated" for the cost estimate. The allocation object is defined in the Object column and is the same as for the recalibration row. Although this example uses a constant, fixed quantities can also be calculated using functions.

2.7.3 A-100 quality inspection

Item 7 of the cost estimate (❹) is the allocated quality inspection time. The amount of time associated with quality inspection differs depending on two things. The first is the number of components in the BOM. Each component must be inspected. The second is whether or not the material is considered a dangerous good. Materials that are not considered dangerous require 30 seconds per component for inspection. Those that are considered dangerous require 1 minute per component. The quality inspection portion of the template has two possible allocations. The first allocation row is labeled "Standard Inspection". The activation for this row is shown in Figure 2.24.

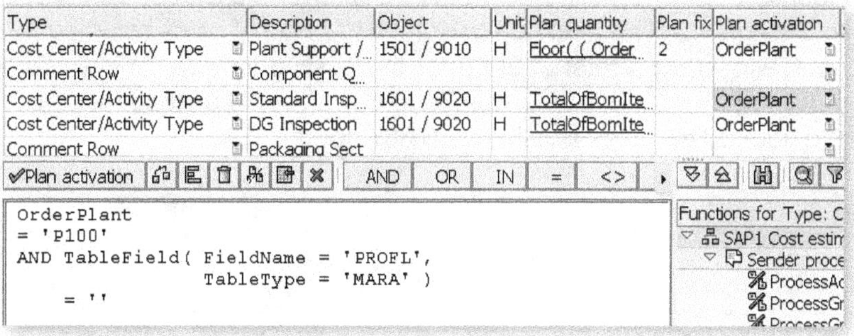

Type		Description	Object	Unit	Plan quantity	Plan fix	Plan activation	
Cost Center/Activity Type	⧉	Plant Support /	1501 / 9010	H	Floor((Order	2	OrderPlant	⧉
Comment Row		⧉ Component Q						⧉
Cost Center/Activity Type	⧉	Standard Insp	1601 / 9020	H	TotalOfBomIte		OrderPlant	⧉
Cost Center/Activity Type	⧉	DG Inspection	1601 / 9020	H	TotalOfBomIte		OrderPlant	⧉
Comment Row		⧉ Packaging Sect						⧉

✔Plan activation | 🔓 | 📧 | 🗑 | 🔍 | 📑 | ✖ | | AND | OR | IN | = | <> | ▸ | ▽ 🔺 | 🔼 🔽 | 🔍 ▽

```
OrderPlant
= 'P100'
AND TableField( FieldName = 'PROFL',
                TableType = 'MARA' )
    = ''
```

Functions for Type: C
▽ 🔩 SAP1 Cost estim
▽ 🔌 Sender proce
% ProcessAc
% ProcessGr
% ProcessGr

Figure 2.24: Standard inspection activation

The value of the field MARA-PROFL (dangerous goods profile) is returned using function TableField and is checked to confirm that no value is assigned. Because the material does not have a value assigned to the dangerous goods profile, this row is enabled.

The second possible allocation for dangerous goods inspection is labeled "DG Inspection". The activation for the DG Inspection row is shown in Figure 2.25. This method expects a value in the dangerous goods profile field, and because there is no value assigned to material A-100, this row is not activated.

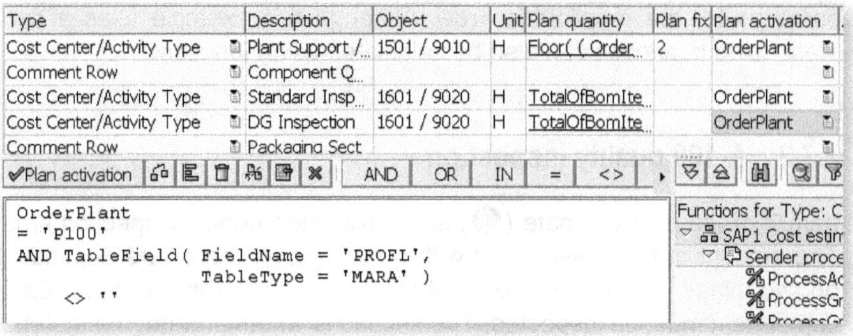

Type	Description	Object	Unit	Plan quantity	Plan fix	Plan activation	
Cost Center/Activity Type	▫ Plant Support /	1501 / 9010	H	Floor((Order	2	OrderPlant	▫
Comment Row	▫ Component Q						▫
Cost Center/Activity Type	▫ Standard Insp	1601 / 9020	H	TotalOfBomIte		OrderPlant	▫
Cost Center/Activity Type	▫ DG Inspection	1601 / 9020	H	TotalOfBomIte		OrderPlant	▫
Comment Row	▫ Packaging Sect						▫

| ✔Plan activation | 🔓 | 🖹 | 🗑 | 🖧 | 🖳 | ✖ | | AND | OR | IN | = | <> | , | 🗟 | 🔺 | 🔡 | 🔍 | 🖅 |

```
OrderPlant
= 'P100'
AND TableField( FieldName = 'PROFL',
                TableType = 'MARA' )
     <> ''
```

Functions for Type: C
▽ 🔓 SAP1 Cost estim
 ▽ 🖳 Sender proce
  % ProcessAc
  % ProcessGr
  % ProcessGr

Figure 2.25: Dangerous goods inspection activation

The formula for the standard inspection (see Figure 2.26) looks for the number of items in the BOM to determine how much of the quality inspection activity should be allocated to the cost estimate. The formula takes the costing lot size and multiplies it by a value returned by the flexible function `TotalOfBomItems`. Flexible functions are described in detail in Section 4.3. The total number of bill of material items returned is 2 for each widget, or a total of 2000 for the costing lot size. This value is then divided by 120, which is used to convert the 30 second inspection time to hours. This gives a value of 16.667 hours.

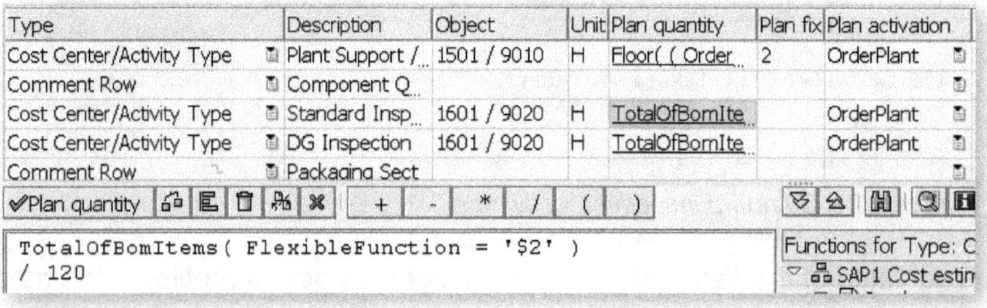

Type	Description	Object	Unit	Plan quantity	Plan fix	Plan activation	
Cost Center/Activity Type	▫ Plant Support /	1501 / 9010	H	Floor((Order	2	OrderPlant	▫
Comment Row	▫ Component Q						▫
Cost Center/Activity Type	▫ Standard Insp	1601 / 9020	H	TotalOfBomIte		OrderPlant	▫
Cost Center/Activity Type	▫ DG Inspection	1601 / 9020	H	TotalOfBomIte		OrderPlant	▫
Comment Row	▫ Packaging Sect						▫

| ✔Plan quantity | 🔓 | 🖹 | 🗑 | 🖧 | ✖ | | + | - | * | / | (|) | | 🗟 | 🔺 | 🔡 | 🔍 | 🗎 |

```
TotalOfBomItems( FlexibleFunction = '$2' )
/ 120
```

Functions for Type: C
▽ 🔓 SAP1 Cost estim

Figure 2.26: Standard inspection formula

The allocation object is cost center 1601 and activity type 9020. This is defined in the method used for object determination, as shown in Figure 2.27.

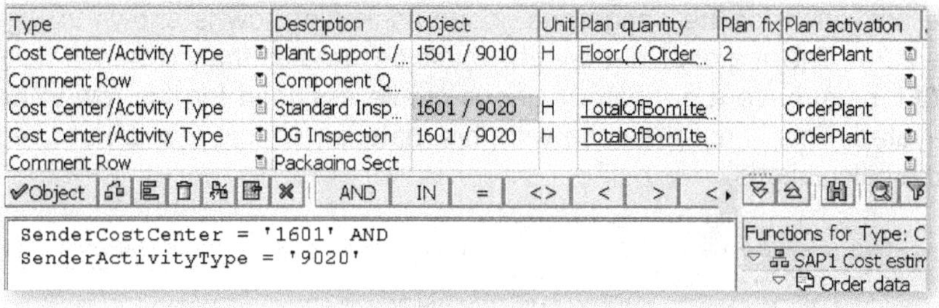

Type	Description	Object	Unit	Plan quantity	Plan fix	Plan activation	
Cost Center/Activity Type	Plant Support /	1501 / 9010	H	Floor((Order	2	OrderPlant	
Comment Row	Component Q						
Cost Center/Activity Type	Standard Insp	1601 / 9020	H	TotalOfBomIte		OrderPlant	
Cost Center/Activity Type	DG Inspection	1601 / 9020	H	TotalOfBomIte		OrderPlant	
Comment Row	Packaging Sect						

Object		AND	IN	=	<>	<	>	<,					

```
SenderCostCenter = '1601' AND
SenderActivityType = '9020'
```

Functions for Type: C
- SAP1 Cost estim
- Order data

Figure 2.27: Standard inspection object determination

2.7.4 A-100 packaging costs

Item 8 of the cost estimate (❺) represents the packaging costs. 17 pal-lets are assigned to the cost estimate. This is represented by 17 EA of business process BP001. Figure 2.19 previously showed the MANU-FACT template, with the section for packaging costs using the subtem-plate WDGTPACK. There are two allocation rows in the template. The first uses BP001 as the object and the second uses BP002 as the object. The plan activation for the first business process row is the method shown in Figure 2.28. If the material net weight is greater than 0 and the dangerous goods indicator (field MARA-PROFL) is unassigned, then this line is activated. Here, the material net weight is 4.1 and MARA-PROFL is blank on the BASIC 2 tab of the material master, so this template row will be processed.

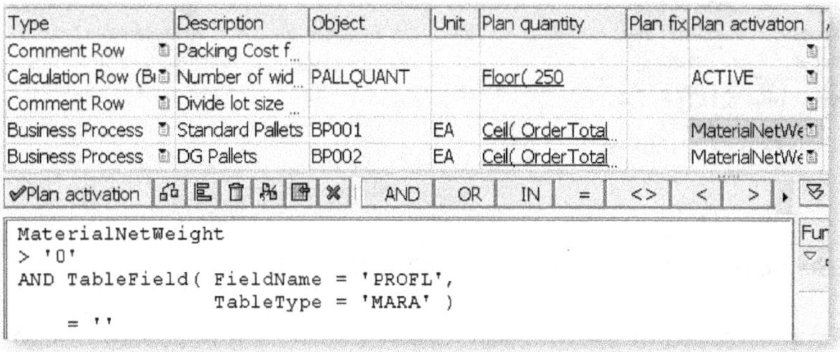

Type	Description	Object	Unit	Plan quantity	Plan fix	Plan activation	
Comment Row	Packing Cost f						
Calculation Row (B	Number of wid	PALLQUANT		Floor(250		ACTIVE	
Comment Row	Divide lot size						
Business Process	Standard Pallets	BP001	EA	Ceil(OrderTotal		MaterialNetWe	
Business Process	DG Pallets	BP002	EA	Ceil(OrderTotal		MaterialNetWe	

Plan activation		AND	OR	IN	=	<>	<	>	,	

```
MaterialNetWeight
> '0'
AND TableField( FieldName = 'PROFL',
                TableType = 'MARA' )
    = ''
```

Fur

Figure 2.28: Activation for standard packaging

The activation for the dangerous goods packaging row is shown in Figure 2.29. The material net weight must be greater than 0 and MARA-PROFL must have a dangerous goods profile assigned for this row to be activated. This is not the case with this material, so this row is not used in the calculations.

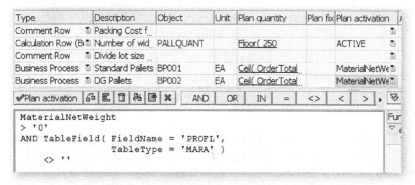

Type	Description	Object	Unit	Plan quantity	Plan fix	Plan activation	
Comment Row	Packing Cost f...						
Calculation Row (B...	Number of wid...	PALLQUANT		Floor(250		ACTIVE	
Comment Row	Divide lot size ...						
Business Process	Standard Pallets	BP001	EA	Ceil(OrderTotal...		MaterialNetWe...	
Business Process	DG Pallets	BP002	EA	Ceil(OrderTotal...		MaterialNetWe...	

Plan activation   AND   OR   IN   =   <>   <   >

```
MaterialNetWeight
> '0'
AND TableField( FieldName = 'PROFL',
                TableType = 'MARA' )
    <> ''
```

Figure 2.29: Activation for special packaging

The formula used in the calculation of the quantity of business process BP001 to allocate to the cost estimate is shown in Figure 2.30. The order quantity is divided by the result of function CalculationRowResult, which refers to the calculation row PALLQUANT.

Type	Description	Object	Unit	Plan quantity	Plan fix	Plan activation	
Comment Row	Packing Cost f...						
Calculation Row (B...	Number of wid...	PALLQUANT		Floor(250		ACTIVE	
Comment Row	Divide lot size ...						
Business Process	Standard Pallets	BP001	EA	Ceil(OrderTotal...		MaterialNetWe...	
Business Process	DG Pallets	BP002	EA	Ceil(OrderTotal...		MaterialNetWe...	

Plan quantity   +   -   *   /   (   )

```
Ceil( OrderTotalQuantity
      / CalculationRowResult( CalculationRowName = 'PALLQUANT'
                              Column = CurrentColumn ) )
```

Figure 2.30: Formula for plan quantity allocation of BP001

The column selected in the function (CurrentColumn) indicates that the formula from PALLQUANT should also come from the plan quantity column. This formula is shown in Figure 2.31.

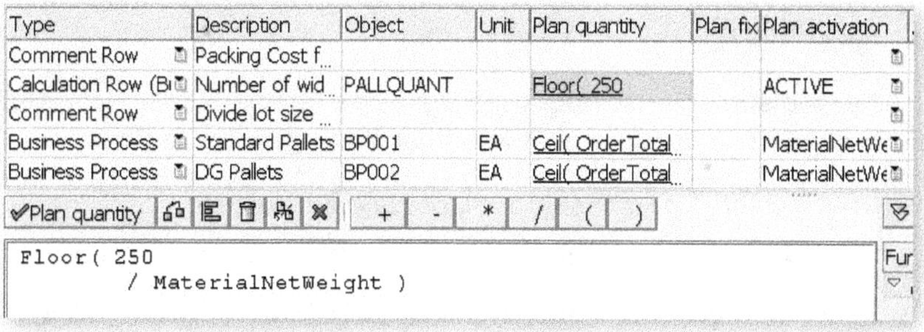

Type		Description	Object	Unit	Plan quantity	Plan fix	Plan activation	
Comment Row		Packing Cost f						
Calculation Row (Bı		Number of wid	PALLQUANT		Floor(250		ACTIVE	
Comment Row		Divide lot size						
Business Process		Standard Pallets	BP001	EA	Ceil(OrderTotal		MaterialNetWe	
Business Process		DG Pallets	BP002	EA	Ceil(OrderTotal		MaterialNetWe	

Plan quantity | + | - | * | / | (|)

```
Floor( 250
        / MaterialNetWeight )
```
Fur

Figure 2.31: Formula from calculation row PALLQUANT

The maximum allowed pallet weight is first divided by the net weight to determine the number of EA that can fit on a pallet. The Floor function is applied to that. Floor always rounds the result down to the previous whole number. The calculated number of widgets is 60.98. Because this is not a whole number, it is rounded down to 60. This represents the number of widgets that can safely be loaded onto one pallet. The costing lot size represented by OrderTotalQuantity is then divided by the result of PALLQUANT. The result is 16.667. This is the number of pallets required to hold 1,000 A-100 widgets. However, partial pallets do not make sense, so the quantity is rounded up to the next whole number (Ceil function). This gives a value of 17. Business process BP001, used to represent packing onto standard pallets, is defined in the Object determination column, as shown in Figure 2.32.

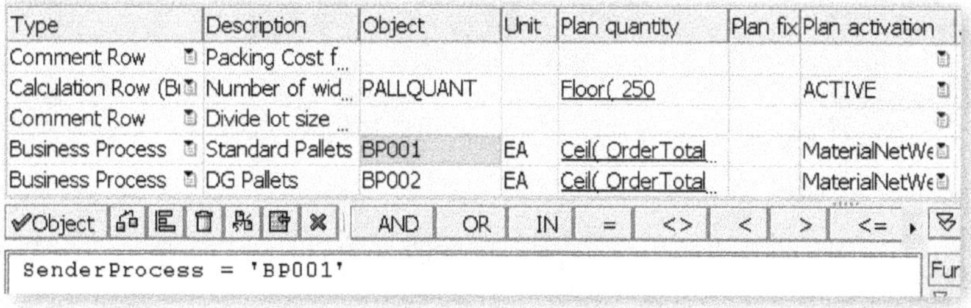

Type		Description	Object	Unit	Plan quantity	Plan fix	Plan activation	
Comment Row		Packing Cost f						
Calculation Row (Bı		Number of wid	PALLQUANT		Floor(250		ACTIVE	
Comment Row		Divide lot size						
Business Process		Standard Pallets	BP001	EA	Ceil(OrderTotal		MaterialNetWe	
Business Process		DG Pallets	BP002	EA	Ceil(OrderTotal		MaterialNetWe	

Object | AND | OR | IN | = | <> | < | > | <= |

```
SenderProcess = 'BP001'
```
Fur

Figure 2.32: Standard packaging business process

2.7.5 Comparing other cost estimates

Two other materials are costed using the same template. Material A-200 is a non-dangerous goods widget with the following characteristics:

▶ net weight: 7.5 kg (BASIC 1 tab of material master)

▶ dangerous goods profile: blank (BASIC 2 tab of material master)

▶ overhead group and key: WIDGET (COSTING 1 tab of material master)

▶ costing lot size: 1,000 (COSTING 1 tab of material master)

▶ number of BOM items: 3 (B-100, B-101, and B-102, coming from the BOM maintenance)

Figure 2.33 shows the resulting cost estimate. Setup and recalibration are the same as for A-100, because the same costing lot size was used for A-200. Quality inspection time is 25 hours for the 1,000 widgets. 3,000 total components are inspected at 30 seconds each. This equates to 1,500 minutes (25 hours). The standard pallet business process is chosen because the dangerous goods profile is blank. The quantity of pallets is calculated by dividing 250 by 7.5 kg to get 33.333. This is rounded down to 33 to get a whole number of widgets per pallet. The costing lot size 1,000 is divided by 30 to give a value of 30.303. This needs to be rounded up to 31, to give a whole number of pallets.

Costing Data	Dates	Qty Struct.	Valuation	History	Costs

Costs Based On   Costing Lot Size   1,000

Itemization for material A-200 in plant P100

ItmNo	I	Resource			Cost Element	▫	Total Value	Currncy	Quantity	Un
1	E	1301	WMAKER	1000	943001		10,000.00	USD	50.00	H
2	E	1301	WMAKER	2000	943002		3,500.00	USD	100.00	H
3	M	P100 B-100			400000		5,000.00	USD	1,000	EA
4	M	P100 B-101			400000		9,000.00	USD	1,000	EA
5	M	P100 B-102			400000		7,500.00	USD	1,000	EA
6	E	1501		9010	943160		337.50	USD	4.50	H
7	E	1501		9010	943160		150.00	USD	2.00	H
8	E	1601		9020	943170		1,125.00	USD	25.00	H
9	X	BP001			943100		310.00	USD	31	EA
						▪	36,922.50	USD		

Figure 2.33: A-200 cost estimate itemization

Material A-300 has the following characteristics:

▶ net weight: 5 kg (BASIC 1 tab of material master)

▶ dangerous goods profile: G01 (BASIC 2 tab of material master)

▶ overhead group and key: WIDGET (COSTING 1 tab of material master)

▶ costing lot size: 10,000 (COSTING 1 tab of material master)

▶ number of BOM items: 3 (2 EA of B-100 and 1 EA of B-102)

		Costing Data	Dates	Qty Struct.	Valuation	History	Costs	

Costs Based On   Costing Lot Size   10,000   EA

Itemization for material A-300 in plant P100

ItmNo	I	Resource			Cost Element	E	Total Value	Currncy	Quantity	Un
1	E	1301	WMAKER	1000	943001		100,000.00	USD	500.00	H
2	E	1301	WMAKER	2000	943002		35,000.00	USD	1,000.00	H
3	M	P100 B-100			400000		100,000.00	USD	20,000	EA
4	M	P100 B-102			400000		75,000.00	USD	10,000	EA
5	E	1501		9010	943160		3,712.50	USD	49.50	H
6	E	1501		9010	943160		150.00	USD	2.00	H
7	E	1601		9020	943170		22,500.00	USD	500.00	H
8	X	BP002			943100		5,000.00	USD	200	EA
							▪ 341,362.	USD		

Figure 2.34: A-300 cost estimate itemization

Figure 2.34 is the resulting cost estimate for A-300 using a costing lot size of 10,000. The change in costing lot size has had an impact on the item 5 recalibration cost. Taking the first 100 away from the 10,000 leaves 9,900 EA, which is equivalent to 99 recalibrations. That is multiplied by 0.5 to give 49.5 hours. The setup remains the same at 2 hours, because this is a fixed quantity that only occurs per order. The ratio between recalibrations and setups has changed significantly due to the larger lot size. The quality inspections shown for item 7 are impacted by two pieces of data. First, the dangerous goods profile is set to G01, indicating that 1 minute is required for each inspection. Second, the number of components is 3. Therefore, 3 inspections x 1 minute x 10,000 widgets gives a total of 30,000 minutes of inspection, which is equivalent to 500 hours. The widget weight is 5 kg, and 50 widgets can fit on a pallet. No rounding is necessary because 250 divided by 5 gives a whole number.

10,000 total widgets divided by 50 gives 200 pallets. Because A-300 has a dangerous goods profile, the BP002 DG Pallet business process is used.

The three cost estimates use different costing lot sizes, therefore the costs for each are not directly comparable. The price unit for all three materials is the same (100) and selecting cost based on that is more effective to show the impact of the template calculations. When converting from the COSTING LOT SIZE view to the PRICE UNIT view, CK11N merely scales down the costs, as shown in Figure 2.35. Only those costing items that were generated using the template are shown for each of the materials.

| Costs Based On | | | Price Unit | | 100 | | |

Itemization for material A-100 in plant P100

ItmNo	I	Resource		Cost Element	Total Value	Currncy	Quantity	Un
5	E	1501	9010	943160	33.75	USD	0.45	H
6	E	1501	9010	943160	15.00	USD	0.20	H
7	E	1601	9020	943170	75.00	USD	1.667	H
8	X	BP001		943100	17.00	USD	1.700	EA

❶

Itemization for material A-200 in plant P100

ItmNo	I	Resource		Cost Element	Total Value	Currncy	Quantity	Un
6	E	1501	9010	943160	33.75	USD	0.45	H
7	E	1501	9010	943160	15.00	USD	0.20	H
8	E	1601	9020	943170	112.50	USD	2.50	H
9	X	BP001		943100	31.00	USD	3.100	EA

❷

Itemization for material A-300 in plant P100

ItmNo	I	Resource		Cost Element	Total Value	Currncy	Quantity	Un
5	E	1501	9010	943160	37.13	USD	0.495	H
6	E	1501	9010	943160	1.50	USD	0.02	H
7	E	1601	9020	943170	225.00	USD	5.00	H
8	X	BP002		943100	50.00	USD	2	EA

❸

Figure 2.35: Comparison of the cost estimates using price unit 100

Comparing the first two materials A-100 and A-200 (cost estimates ❶ and ❷), the setup and recalibration costs in the first two items are the same. This is because they use the same costing lot size. A difference shows up in the third item (quality inspection) that is based on the number of components for each widget: 2 for A-100 versus 3 for A-200. The final comparison item is the packaging costs. Both use business process BP001 for standard pallets, but the quantity is different due to the difference in the net weight for each material.

A-300 (cost estimate ❸) shows the impact of the larger costing lot size and the dangerous goods profile assigned to it. The lot size affects both the number of hours associated with recalibration as well as the relative impact of the setup cost. The adjusted recalibration hours are 0.495 compared to 0.45, and the adjusted setup is 0.02 hours versus 0.2 hours. The lot size affected these costs. Even though the actual setup cost is the same and the overall recalibration costs are more for A-300, the costs per unit are lower than for either A-100 and A-200. Quality inspection costs per unit for A-300 are double the quality inspection costs for material A-200, even though they both have 3 components. The dangerous goods profile assigned to A-300 dictated that each inspection should be twice as long than for either of the other two materials. The last item shows the packaging costs. Even though A-300 only requires two pallets per price unit and A-200 requires 3.1, the cost is much higher for A-300 due to the dangerous goods profile. That profile dictated that business process BP002 be used for DG pallets and handling, which has a higher price than the standard pallet business process BP001.

3 Templates in cost object controlling

Chapter 2 introduced details of the structure of templates using product costing as an example. The true power of these structures is manifested in the various methods and formulas that are used to generate allocations specific to the characteristics defined for the receiving cost objects. ABAP functions and values from table fields available in the environment are used to determine the circumstances that cause an allocation to be triggered, and they are also used in the formulas for calculating the quantity of that allocation. Learning how to create these methods and formulas is key to unlocking the power of templates.

3.1 Production scenario

Chapter 2 introduced template structures and how they are used in a planning environment. The same templates can be used to perform actual allocations as well as plan allocations. This chapter uses the same scenario, focusing on actual allocations for production orders. It covers the maintenance of the methods and formulas used in the allocation calculations. Plant P100 makes widgets. Some of these widgets are considered "dangerous goods", which affects the quality inspection and packaging for shipment. Material A-100 is one of the widgets for which cost estimates were created using templates for plan allocation. The production orders associated with manufacturing these widgets must account for the actual setup time, recalibration time, quality inspection time, and palletizing that make up the special activities associated with these materials.

Production planning has created an order to manufacture 1,455 EA of widget A-100, which is not classified as a dangerous good. The order number is 60003992 and is shown in Figure 3.1.

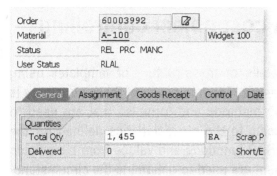

Figure 3.1: Order for material A-100

When processing the order, 60 EA were scrapped due to problems that occurred during the assembly process. 1,455 widgets were shipped to the customer. The order should account for the following activity quantities:

- ▶ 2 hours of set up time

- ▶ 7 hours of recalibration time from a total of 1,515 good and bad widgets processed (After the 100th widget is produced, recalibration begins, and takes place every 100 widgets thereafter. The last calibration would have been performed at widget 1,500. Each recalibration takes 0.5 hours, so the total recalibration hours are calculated as follows: 1,500 minus 100, divided by 100, and then multiplied by 0.5 hours.)

- ▶ 25.25 hours of inspection time (1,515 widgets multiplied by 2 components multiplied by 30 seconds, converted to hours)

- ▶ 25 standard pallets and associated costs for packing the widgets on the pallets (1,455 widgets divided by 60 widgets per pallet, based on 4.1 kg per widget and 250 kg per pallet, rounded up to the next whole pallet)

3.2   Defining the templates

Production orders use the same 001 environment as product cost estimates. Therefore, the same template can be used for both the allocation of plan costs to the cost estimate as well as for the allocation of actual costs. Environment 001 has the provision for the allocation of both types of costs using the same allocation objects for each. There is a specific activation for plan allocations and another one for actual allocations. This is because the characteristics used for determining and calculating the plan allocations are likely different than those which are used for actual allocations. Figure 3.2 shows the MANUFACT template from Chapter 2, updated for actual allocations.

| Template | MANUFACT | Manufacturing |
| Environment | 001 | Cost estimate/production orders |

Template overview : display

Type	Description	Object	Unit	Plan quantity	Plan fix	Plan activation	Actual quantity	Actual fix	Actual activ	Actual alloc
Comment Row	Template for									
Comment Row	Machine Setup									
Cost Center/Activit	Plant Support /	1501 / 9010	H	Floor((Order	2	OrderPlant	Floor((Order	2	OrderPlant	
Comment Row	Component Q									
Cost Center/Activit	Standard Insp	SenderCostCent		TotalOfBomIte		OrderPlant	(OrderYieldCo		OrderPlant	
Cost Center/Activit	DG Inspection	1601 / 9020	H	TotalOfBomIte		OrderPlant	(OrderYieldCo		OrderPlant	
Comment Row	Packaging Sect									
Subtemplate	Widget Packing	WDGTPACK				MaterialNetWe				

Figure 3.2: MANUFACT template with actual columns

The WDGTPACK subtemplate has also been updated to process actual allocations (see Figure 3.3).

| Template | WDGTPACK | Widget Packing |
| Environment | 001 | Cost estimate/production orders |

Template overview : change

Description	Object	Unit	Plan quantity	Plan fix	Plan activation	Actual quantity	Actual fix	Actual activation	Actual allocatio
Packing Cost f									
Number of wid	PALLQUANT		Floor(250		ACTIVE	Floor(250		ACTIVE	
Divide lot size									
Standard Pallets	SenderProcess		Cell(OrderTot		MaterialNetWe	Cell(OrderTo		MaterialNetWe	OrderShipment
DG Pallets	SenderProcess		Cell(OrderTot		MaterialNetWe	Cell(OrderTo		MaterialNetWe	OrderShipment

Figure 3.3: WDGTPACK template with actual columns

The following sections define how to enter the methods and formulas used for both plan and actual allocations.

3.3 Template methods

A *method* is a procedure that returns a value which controls how the template row is used in calculations. Methods are used in object determination, activation, and allocation events. They can return different types of values depending on purpose. A Boolean value (true/false) is returned from methods used for activation purposes. A value representing an allocation object is returned from methods used for object determination, and a numeric value is returned from allocation event methods to indicate the fiscal period in which the allocation should take place.

3.3.1 Methods for activation

Activation expects a Boolean result to determine if the row should be active. This can be accomplished in two ways. First, the method could be made up of a Boolean type function, which returns a value of either true or false, depending on the parameters passed to it. The second way is to compare two values. The comparison results in a value of either true or false, satisfying the requirements for an activation method.

Comparisons have three parts. The first part is a function that returns a value retrieved from the available data in the environment. The second part is a relational operator used to define what comparison is being made. The allowed operators are: = (equals), <> (not equal), < (less than), > (greater than), <= (less than or equal to), and >= (greater than or equal to). Following the operator, there is a function or a literal value enclosed in quotation marks. The comparison is made between the two operands using the middle operator. A special operator, IN, is used to search an array of values to determine if the first operand is contained within that group. This can either be an array of literal values enclosed in quotation marks, or it can be a special function that returns a group of values. If the value of the first operand is found in the group, then a value of true is returned. Arithmetic operators are not allowed in comparisons.

Comparisons in activation

 A business process row should be activated when the plant on the order is P010. One way to approach this is to use a literal constant for plant P010 in the comparison. The method looks like this: OrderPlant = 'P010'. A different way to handle this is to see if the order plant matches the plant assigned to the business process. In this case, a function that returns the plant of the business process is used instead of the literal.

OrderPlant = SenderProcessPlant activates the row if the plant assigned to the business process matches the plant for the order. Finally,

---

the IN operator can be used to check for the value of the plant in the order. This could be expressed as `OrderPlant IN ( 'P005', 'P010', 'P011', 'P012' )`. Because P010 is in the list, the row is activated.

Two or more comparisons can be linked together using the Boolean logical operators `AND` and `OR`. Each comparison is evaluated on its own and then the result for each is further processed with the logical operators used. The `AND` operator only returns a value of true if both comparisons return a value of true. Otherwise, the value returned is false. The `OR` operator only returns a value of false if both comparisons return a value of false. Otherwise, it returns a value of true. Methods with multiple comparisons can make use of both the `AND` and the `OR` operators. The expressions are generally evaluated from left to right, but `AND` operators are processed before `OR` operators. Parentheses can be used to control the order of the evaluation of the expression. The expressions enclosed in parentheses are evaluated first. The use of parentheses can be nested. In this case, the expression within the innermost set of parentheses is evaluated first, and then the next level is evaluated.

Using parentheses in complex comparisons

Parentheses can help make sure that the proper result is returned from a complex method, as shown in the following example:

An activation method contains three comparisons: A, B, and C. Comparison A returns a value of true, comparison B also returns true, and C is false. The `AND` operator is always processed before the `OR` operator. The expression A `OR` B `AND` C gives a value of true. The value of B `AND` C is false because at least one of the comparisons is false. This result is used in the `OR` operation with A, which gives a value of true, because A is true. When parentheses are added, the results can be different. The expression (A `OR` B) `AND` C gives a value of false. A `OR` B is evaluated first and has a value of true because A and B are both true. The `AND` operator looks at this result along with the value of C. Because C is false, the value of the expression is also false. It is always best to use parentheses in complex comparisons to make sure the desired result is returned.

3.3.2   Creating the activation method

Select the activation cell for the row. The Actual Allocation cell controls whether the actual quantity allocation is performed and the Plan Allocation cell controls the plan quantity allocation. There is a dropdown menu for this cell which contains the choices ACTIVE and INACTIVE. Choosing either of these permanently activates or deactivates the actual calculation row without regard to any parameters available to the environment. The function `Activation = 'ACTIVE'` or `Activation = 'INACTIVE'` is automatically loaded as the method. If the requirement for the row looks at data available in the environment to determine if the row should be enabled, it is necessary to create a more complex method. Double click in the cell or click on the ⬚ button to open the method editing area at the bottom of the main window.

Based on the scenario, the method for determining whether to allocate the standard quality inspection activity quantities is based on the plant being P100 and the dangerous goods profile in the material master being blank. Figure 3.4 shows what the editing window looks like when first entering. It is divided into two sections. The blank section is where the method is entered. The right section has a list of template functions available for ACTUAL ACTIVATION.

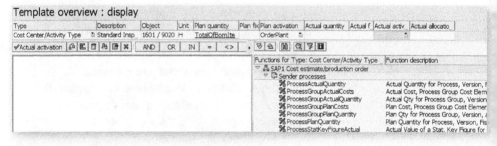

Figure 3.4: Actual activation edit window

Two sets of icons are at the top of the method editing section. One set controls editing features and the other contains the list of operators available to use in the method. The operator buttons insert the specified operator in the method and automatically separate the operator with spaces. The list of activation icons is long and may not completely fit above the window. Arrow buttons (▶ and ◀) are used to scroll right and left through the list of icons.

The method is created by using functions copied from the function window. A function can be copied to the edit window in one of three ways. The first is to select the function with the mouse and drag the function to the edit window. Another way is to click on the function and then click on the ⬧ button to move the function. A third option is to double click on the function to move it to the edit window. If the selected function requires parameters, a window is displayed so that the parameters can be assigned to the function. A relational operator is required after the function is selected. Proper syntax requires a space between the function and the operator. Using one of the operator buttons at the top of the edit window automatically inserts the space. All operators except the Boolean AND and OR can be used at this point. After the operator, there needs to be either a constant or another function that returns a value, in order to define the condition to be checked. To check compound conditions, the AND or the OR operator can be selected. These can either be typed or selected by using the corresponding button.

The other buttons at the top of the function window can aid in determining which function to use. The ⬧ button restricts the list of functions to only those that can be used at the point where the cursor is displayed in the edit window. Certain functions can only be used at specific points in a method and result in a method error if assigned to the wrong place. The ⬧ button returns the documentation for the selected function, making it easier to understand how to use that function. The arrow buttons ⬧ ⬧ can open and close specific structure nodes and function trees in the function window. The ⬧ button is used to find a specific function based on the string that is entered.

Once a function is selected, the system looks at the function definition to determine if parameters are required. If no parameters are required, the function is copied into the edit window at a place pointed to by the cursor. If parameters are required, an additional window is displayed for entering them. Figure 3.5 shows the result of selecting the TableField function. This function is used to return a specific field from one of the tables or structures available to the environment. This function has two parameters. If the OPTIONAL column has a check mark in it for a given parameter, then it is not necessary to enter a value for that parameter. However, any value that is entered for those parameters can help narrow down the results of the function. Any parameter where OPTIONAL has no check mark must have a value entered. A parameter can be literal or can be the result of another function call. The list of functions is displayed below the parameters. Not all functions return a value that is compatible with a specific parameter, so care should be taken to select a meaningful function.

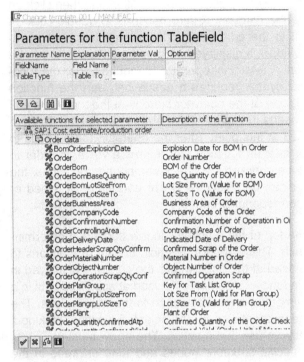

Figure 3.5: Function parameters

This specific activation method needs to get the value for the dangerous goods profile from the material master table MARA. This is the PROFL field, and it is entered between the quotation marks in the first parameter value cell. The table name is the second parameter, and MARA should be entered there. Once the parameters have been entered, press the [Enter] key or click on the ✔ button to move the function to the edit window. The scenario requires confirmation that the plant is P100 and the material has not been assigned a dangerous goods profile. First, the OrderPlant function is selected and the = operator is used to check for a match with the literal 'P100'. There is no function currently defined to return the dangerous goods profile, so the TableField function is selected to return its value. Prior to selecting the function, choose the AND operator to connect the two functions, indicating that both conditions must be true for the row to be activated. Figure 3.6 shows the method after the functions have been selected and operations defined.

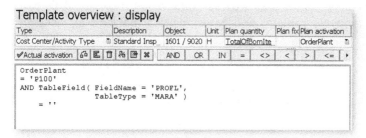

Figure 3.6: Method before cleaning

The display at this point is somewhat messy and hard to read. Click on the 🗈 button to view a more readable display. Figure 3.7 shows the result of cleaning up the display.

Template overview : display

OrderPlant
= 'P100'
AND TableField(FieldName = 'PROFL',
                TableType = 'MARA')
    = ''

Figure 3.7: Method after cleaning

A preliminary syntax check is performed first. If there are errors, these must be fixed prior to cleaning up the text in the window. Another way of checking syntax is to click on the 🔍 button. This also highlights errors in the syntax of the method or formula. Once it is determined that the method is complete, click on ✓Actual activation to save the method. There is a button like this for every method or formula cell, and it should be used if changes are made. The other edit buttons can also be very useful. The 🔣 button is "undo". Clicking on this button deletes any typing that has been done since the method was last saved. The 🗑 button is used to delete the entire method. The ✖ button cancels any changes that have been made and returns to the state that existed prior to entering the edit window. The final button is 🗃 . This is used bring up a selection window for values that can be used. For example, if the exact plant ID is not known after entering OrderPlant =, click on 🗃 to get a list of possible plants. This operation is context specific, based on the function, and may not be available in all cases. This is only for methods which use functions that are used for comparison with specific objects.

> ### Using material characteristics
>
> Perhaps one of the most useful sources of data for activation methods and object determination methods is material characteristics. Material characteristics extend the standard set of fields in the material master to provide a much wider array of values accessible to templates. Two functions are provided for checking and using characteristic values in formulas and methods. `MaterialCharValueExists` is used to check if the specified characteristic is assigned to the material. This is used for activation purposes. Once it is determined that the characteristic is available, `MaterialCharacteristicValue` can be used to return the value of the specific characteristic. This can be used in quantity formulas as well as in activation methods. This can greatly extend the amount and types of data that can be used in templates.

3.3.3 Methods for object determination

Methods are also used in object determination. In this case, the result cannot be a true/false result, but must return values that can be used as allocation objects for the specific row type. The objects for a business process row must be business processes, and the objects for a cost center/activity type row must be cost centers with activity types. The result can be one object or a list of objects. If more than one object is returned, the quantity calculated for the row applies to each object that is returned. Using a cost estimate example, if the result of the object determination finds three business processes, then three separate business process items are added to the cost estimate, and each one has the same quantity calculated for it as for the others.

The format of the method requires a function that returns the type allowed by the row, a relational operator, and another function or literal. The allowed relational operators are = (equals), <> (not equal), < (less than), > (greater than), <= (less than or equal to), >= (greater than or equal to), and IN. Mathematical operators are not allowed. Complex conditions can be specified to narrow down the results. These conditions are connected using the Boolean AND and OR operators, as described in Section 3.3.1.

Business process object determination

A simple form of determining which business process to use is to directly specify it by using SenderProcess = 'BP01'. The object selected is BP01. SenderProcess IN ('BP01', 'BP02', 'BP03') returns business processes BP01, BP02, and BP03, if they exist. SenderProcess IN ProcessesInProcessGroup(GroupName = 'CA01') returns all business process that are assigned to business process group CA01. Business processes can be assigned attributes on the ATTRIBUTE tab of the master data maintenance transaction CP02, and these can be used in complex conditions to further specify which business process should be selected from the group. BP01 is assigned attribute BLUE, BP02 is assigned RED, and BP03 is assigned BLUE. Using the AND operator, the method SenderProcess IN ('BP01', 'BP02', 'BP03') AND SenderProcessAttribute1 = 'BLUE' returns business processes BP01 and BP03 as the objects. There are several template functions that can return object IDs without resorting to the use of literals, and this can be a powerful means of making a specific template useable for multiple and variable allocation scenarios.

3.3.4 Creating the object determination method

The same object determination is used for both plan and actual calculations. The methods used for object determination must be valid for both types of allocations. Template MANUFACT uses object determination for cost centers and activity types. A specific cost center and activity type can be entered directly into the object cell for the roll. The format is the cost center ID, space, /, space, activity type. A selection can be made from the dropdown menu for the cell. Figure 3.8 shows 1601 and 9020 highlighted in the OBJECT cell; this is stored as per the method shown in the edit window.

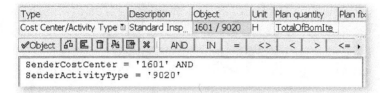

Figure 3.8: Method for object determination

This simple method for defining an allocation object is useful when an explicit sender object is required. However, templates are more powerful when allocations are performed that are common to multiple objects. Figure 3.9 shows a method for selecting a cost center based on a specific cost center group, and an activity type based on combining a series of substrings that can be used to match the ID. The asterisk is used as a wildcard, meaning that at that point in the text, any values can be used.

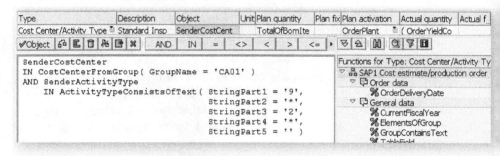

Figure 3.9: Complex method for object determination

The `CostCenterFromGroup` function returns every cost center belonging to group CA01. Because this object type is cost center/activity type, the second part of the method finds the activity type and restricts the result to those cost centers in group CA01 that use that activity type. `ActivityTypeConsistsOfText` returns any activity type that begins with 9 and contains a 2 in the name. The asterisks are used as wild cards and stand for any combination of characters in the string. Therefore, 9020, 9A2BCD, and 9029999 are all valid activity types. In this scenario, only cost center 1601/activity type 9020 fits the pattern. Therefore, this is the only object that is returned. Figure 3.10 shows the result of the allocation in the cost estimate.

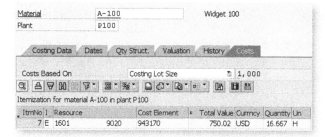

Figure 3.10: Cost center/activity type assignment

Other types of characteristics of the allocation objects can be used to select the objects. This is best illustrated with the business processes from template WDGTPACK. The original methods for the business processes were of the simple type: SenderProcess = 'BP001', which explicitly assigns a specific business process to each of the allocation rows.

Business processes BP001 and BP002 are both assigned to plant P100 and have a couple of attributes assigned. These attributes can be used in object determination. Figure 3.11 shows the tabs in the definition of the business processes BP001 and BP002 which define the characteristics used in the method for object determination.

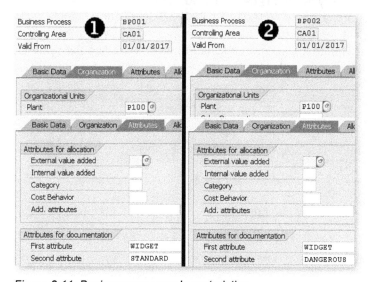

Figure 3.11: Business process characteristics

The WDGTPACK template has been changed to take advantage of the assignment of plant and first attribute. In this case, the values of the plant and attribute 1 are the same for both business processes (see Figure 3.12 and Figure 3.13). The values in the two methods are the same, so this might not be enough to specify one business process over the other.

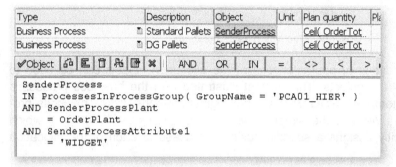

Figure 3.12: Standard packaging object selection

Figure 3.12 shows the selection method for the standard packaging business process using business process group, assigned plant, and attribute 1 set to WIDGET. The first function must return an object of the business process type. In this case, the business process must be in the standard hierarchy group PCA01_HIER. If no other characteristics are used to restrict the selection, all business processes within that group are returned. The next two comparisons are used to reduce the returned set to a specific number of business processes.

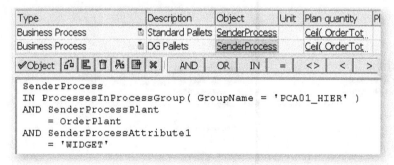

Figure 3.13: Dangerous goods packaging object selection

The first comparison is to check that the plant assigned to the business process matches the plant of the order or cost estimate (SenderProcessPlant = OrderPlant). The second comparison checks the value of the first attribute to see if this business process is associated with widgets (SenderProcessAttribute1 = 'WIDGET'). Only the business processes in group PCA01_HIER with those two characteristics are chosen.

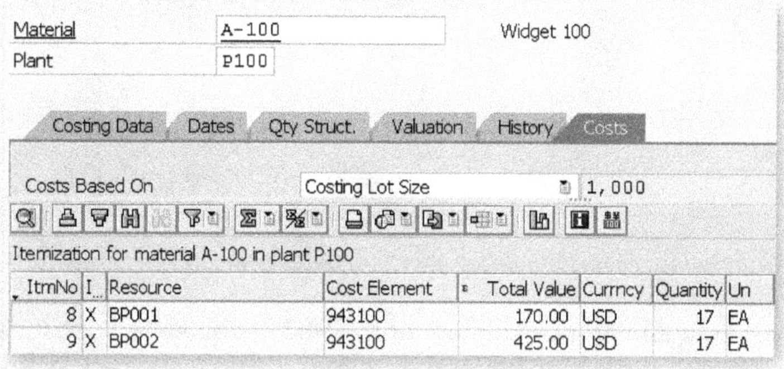

| Material | A-100 | Widget 100 |
| Plant | P100 | |

| | Costing Data | Dates | Qty Struct. | Valuation | History | Costs |

| Costs Based On | | Costing Lot Size | | 1,000 |

Itemization for material A-100 in plant P100

ItmNo	I	Resource	Cost Element	ª	Total Value	Currncy	Quantity	Un
8	X	BP001	943100		170.00	USD	17	EA
9	X	BP002	943100		425.00	USD	17	EA

Figure 3.14: Cost estimate result with two business processes

Looking at the costing result in Figure 3.14, both business processes are found and are included in the cost estimate. This would be the correct result if the requirement called for both business processes to be allocated. However, this scenario differentiates between standard packaging, represented by BP001, and dangerous goods packaging, represented by BP002.

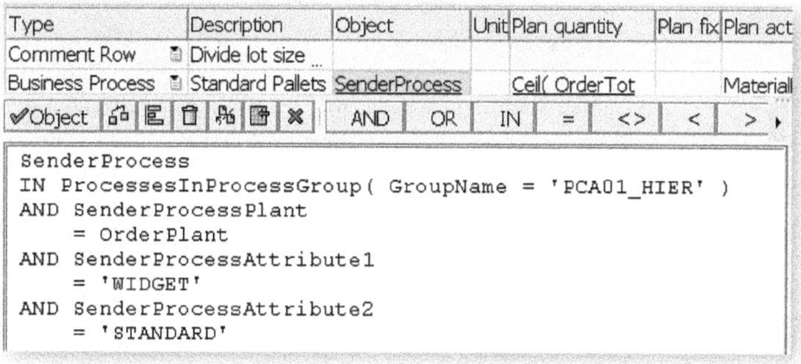

Type	Description	Object	Unit	Plan quantity	Plan fix	Plan act
Comment Row	Divide lot size ...					
Business Process	Standard Pallets	SenderProcess		Ceil(OrderTot		Material

| ✔Object | 🔁 | 📧 | 🗑 | 🔀 | 📋 | ✖ | AND | OR | IN | = | <> | < | > | ▸ |

```
SenderProcess
IN ProcessesInProcessGroup( GroupName = 'PCA01_HIER' )
AND SenderProcessPlant
    = OrderPlant
AND SenderProcessAttribute1
    = 'WIDGET'
AND SenderProcessAttribute2
    = 'STANDARD'
```

Figure 3.15: Updated standard packaging determination

77

Figure 3.15 and Figure 3.16 show the object determination methods with the additional comparison for the second attribute, which is used to segregate the business processes by type of packaging.

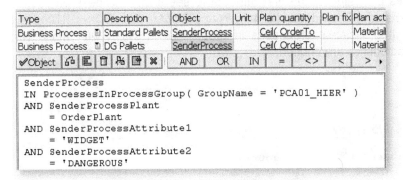

Figure 3.16: Updated dangerous goods packaging determination

When the cost estimate is recalculated, only BP001 is allocated because the material does not have a dangerous goods ID as specified in the activation column for this row. This is shown in Figure 3.17.

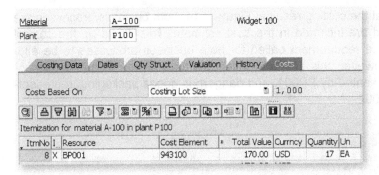

Figure 3.17: Resulting cost with updated object determination

Although the examples in this section use the plan allocation quantities, the same also applies to the actual quantities. The object determination is common for both plan and actual calculations.

3.3.5 Methods for allocation events

Allocation events are only available for environments that belong to the COB application (environments 001 through 012). Cost objects in this application include orders, WBS elements, and networks, among others. These objects exist independently of the fiscal year, and performing allocation to these objects each period is not always appropriate. The allocation event column is used to specify a condition that must apply before the allocation can be made. This ensures that certain allocations can only take place during the period in which the event occurred. Allocation events are usually only applicable to actual allocations and not plan allocations. The exceptions to this are networks and WBS elements (environments 004 and 005), which allow for plan allocation events. Environment 001 is for production orders and material cost estimates. Allocations of actual costs might only occur when an order is complete, which is determined by order status. Plan costs for an order look at the order in its entirety and do not need to be restricted to a time-specific allocation. For this reason, only allocation events for actuals work for orders.

Methods for allocation events are simple and allow no operators. The result is a numeric value representing a period for the allocation. If the period matches the selected period, the allocation is made. Functions available for allocation events must return a numeric value representing the period.

Order actual allocation event

 Overhead costs associated with shipping a product are allocated when the production order has been fully confirmed (status CNF). The actual allocation event used is the OrderEnd function. The order is started in period 3 and is completed in period 5. OrderEnd returns the period number associated with the date when the CNF status is set, otherwise it returns a 0. CNF is set in period 5. The template allocation is run for period 3, 4, and 5, but the template only returns a quantity to allocate during period 5.

3.3.6 Creating the allocation event method

When creating a method for allocation events, no operators are allowed. The function returns a specific condition, which in this case is associated with a specific order status. The three delivered functions are shown in Figure 3.18.

Figure 3.18: Selections for actual allocation events

OrderEnd looks at the time that the CNF (fully confirmed) status is set. OrderShipped looks at the DLV (fully delivered) status. OrdersStart looks at the REL (released) status. Each returns the period in which the status was first set. If the period for the allocation does not match the period returned, the actual allocation will not be performed.

Select the function that matches the order status desired for the allocation. If the allocation occurs regardless of status, the method should remain blank. In this scenario, the allocation for quality inspection should occur based on order confirmations and should not be restricted by status. The same is also true for the setup and recalibration. None of these allocations should wait until the order is complete. The packaging allocation in template WDGTPACK needs to wait until the order is complete, and OrderShipped is selected to restrict this allocation to the time that the order status is changed to DLV.

3.4 Template formulas

A *formula* is a mathematical expression that returns a numeric value. One purpose of the formula is to calculate a quantity of the row object to allocate to the receiver. The simplest form of the formula is a single constant value, such as 3.14. If a constant value is used, it must be a positive number or 0. Negative constants are not allowed. Formulas can be much more complex than that, and they can use a combination of functions, constants, and arithmetic operators to determine a quantity based on the various factors available to the environment. Only functions that return a numeric value can be used as a part of an operand in the calculation. Four operators are supported: + (addition), − (subtraction), * (multiplication), and / (division). These four operators are bolstered by several mathematical functions that are generally available in all template environments. These are:

- ▶ Abs—returns the absolute value (e. g. −4.75 returns 4.75)

- ▶ Ceil—round up to the next higher whole number (e. g. 4.75 returns 5, and −4.75 returns −4)

- ▶ Exp—raises the mathematical constant e (2.718...) to the power of the expression enclosed in the following parentheses. The value returned by Exp(0) is 1, and the value returned by Exp(2) is 7.389.

- ▶ Floor—round down to the next lower whole number (e. g. 4.75 returns 4, and −4.75 returns −5)

- ▶ Frac—returns the fractional part of the number (e. g. 4.75 becomes 0.75, and −4.75 becomes −0.75)

- ▶ Sign—returns the "value" of the sign of the expression (e. g. 4.75 returns 1, and −4.75 returns −1)

- ▶ Sqrt—returns the square root of the expression (e. g. 9 returns 3, and 2 returns 1.414). A negative value results in a calculation error.

- ▶ Trunc—truncates the decimal portion of the value (e. g. 4.75 returns 4, and −4.75 returns −4)

None of the operators allowed for methods can be used in a mathematical formula and are not made available in the formula editor.

Using parentheses in complex formulas

Operators in a formula are processed based on a hierarchy. Multiplication and division are processed first, followed by addition and subtraction. Any operator at the same hierarchy level, such as multiplication and division, are processed from left to right in the formula; for example,

10 + 20 / 5 − 2 without parentheses gives a value of 12. The portion 20 / 5 is determined first and gives a value of 4. This is then added to the 10 to give 14, and 2 is subtracted from that to give 12. When parentheses are added, the portion of the formula in parentheses is processed first regardless of the order. For example, (10 + 20) / 5 - 2 gives a value of 4 (10 + 20 is 30, and 30 divided by 5 is 6, and 6 minus 2 is 4). Alternatively, (10 + 20) / (5 − 2) gives a value of 10 (30 divided by 3). Always make sure that the formula is in the correct order, and that the parentheses are in the proper place.

3.4.1   Creating a template formula

The formula for determining the quantity of products reported by manufacturing order confirmations needs to include both good production and scrapped production. Functions for formulas are selected from the function window in the same manner as for the methods described above. Function OrderYieldConfirmed (see Figure 3.19) returns the value of good production, and OrderHeaderScrapQtyConfirm returns total scrapped production. The sum is used in the calculation of inspection time. This value is divided by 120 to give the total number of hours to allocate, based on an inspection time of 30 seconds per part. This then needs to be multiplied by the number of items in the BOM.

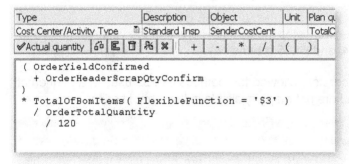

Figure 3.19: Formula for actual quantity

The formula in Figure 3.20 calculates the number of hours required for recalibration after the first 100 widgets have been produced. This is then divided by 100 to calculate the number of recalibrations. The Floor function is used to exclude any fractional part because recalibrations are not required for that portion of the production.

```
Type                            Description    Object        Unit  Plan quantity  Plan fix
Cost Center/Activity Type ▣ Plant Support / 1501 / 9010  H   Floor( ( Order    2
✔Actual quantity  ᠍᠍  ⎒  ⎙  ⍀  ✖    +   -   *   /   (   )

Floor( ( OrderYieldConfirmed
            + OrderHeaderScrapQtyConfirm
          - 100
        )
        / 100 )
  * 0.5
```

Figure 3.20: Formula with special mathematical function

3.5   Connecting the template to the order

The method of connecting the order costs to the template is the same as for product costing. When the production order is created, the overhead key is copied into the order from the material master. The CONTROL tab of the order contains the costing information (see Figure 3.21).

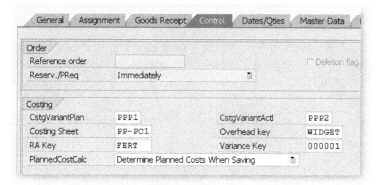

Figure 3.21: Control tab for order from transaction CO02

Two costing variants are normally used in cost calculations for production orders. PPP1 is the costing variant used for calculating the plan costs for the order and uses valuation variant 006. The default costing sheet used in the order is the one assigned to this valuation variant. PPP2 is for simultaneous costing for the order and is used for the actual cost calculations. It uses valuation variant 007. The template must be connected through a costing sheet assigned to each valuation variant.

The same costing sheet should be assigned for both valuation variants so that the templates are accessible for both plan and actual order costs. If a different costing sheet is assigned in the order than is assigned to the valuation variant of the actual costing variant, then the template must be configured for both costing sheets. To prevent confusion, use the same costing sheet for both valuation variants if at all possible. The WIDGET overhead key is copied from the material master definition for product A-100 when the order is created for that material. As in product costing, there needs to be a connection associated with the overhead key to the costing sheet (PP-PC1 in this case) and from there to the template. Figure 3.22 shows this connection using the configuration transaction KTPF (IMG menu option: CONTROLLING • PRODUCT COST CONTROLLING • COST OBJECT CONTROLLING • PRODUCT COST BY ORDER • BASIC SETTINGS FOR PRODUCT COST BY ORDER • TEMPLATES • ASSIGN TEMPLATES TO COST OBJECTS).

Change View "View for Template Determination":

New Entries

COAr	CostSh	OH key	Environ.	Template	Name
CA01	PP-PC1	WIDGET	001	MANUFACT	Manufacturing

Figure 3.22: Assignment of MANUFACT to order valuation variants

When the order is saved, the preliminary cost estimate is created using costing variant PPP1. Figure 3.23 shows the portion of the cost estimate that was generated using template MANUFACT.

Order	60003992 A-100
Material	A-100 Widget 100
Plant	P100 Plant 100
Lot Size	1,455 EA Each
Cost Base	1,455 EA Each

ItmNo	I	Resource	Resource (Text)	Σ	Total Value	COCr	Quantity	Un
6	E	1501	9010 Plant Support / Support Hours		487.50	USD	6.50	H
7	E	1501	9010 Plant Support / Support Hours		150.00	USD	2.00	H
8	E	1601	9020 Plant QC / QC Hours		1,091.25	USD	24.25	H
9	X	BP001	Pack using standard pallets		250.00	USD	25	EA
(not assigned)				Σ	1,978.75	USD		

Figure 3.23: Allocation portion of order plan costs

This cost estimate is generated with the same formulas and methods as those used in the cost estimate in Chapter 2. The resulting quantities in the report are different because the order size is 1,455 widgets instead of the 1,000 widgets used for the standard cost estimate.

3.6 Executing the actual allocation

Plan costs from templates for standard cost estimates and preliminary order cost estimate are automatically determined from the allocation based on the connection of the template. These types of plan costs are "event driven", and the allocation is triggered by the creation of the cost estimate. Actual allocations for orders are processed on a periodic basis and require running a separate allocation transaction, usually as a part of period-end closing. Transactions CPTA and CPTD are used for template allocations for production orders. CPTA is used for a single order, and CPTD is used for all orders for a plant.

Three different events that occurred in order 60003992 are reviewed to examine the effects of actual template allocations at these points in the order life cycle. Order 60003992 is expected to deliver 1,455 EA of material A-100. The first event looks at the results that occur for a template allocation after 800 units have been confirmed in production, with a scrap total of 30. The second event occurs after an additional 655 units, along with 30 more units of scrap, have been confirmed. The final event is the goods receipt of the 1,455 good widgets into inventory, to be made ready for shipment.

First allocation for order 60003992

800 EA of A-100 have been confirmed in manufacturing. 30 additional units have been declared bad after the manufacturing step, and have been scrapped. Order status has been set to PCNF (partially confirmed). At this point in the order, transaction CPTA is run in order to perform the template allocation. Figure 3.24 shows that this transaction is period based and is used to allocate to the specific order.

Controlling Area	CA01	
Order	60003992	
Parameters		
Version	0	Plan/Act - Version
Period	1	To
Fiscal Year	2018	

Figure 3.24: Transaction CPTA

An allocation report can be generated when running CPTA to show the result of the allocation. Figure 3.25 shows the result of the allocation.

Selection

Order	60003992	Widget 100
Version	0	Plan/Act - Version
Fiscal Year	2018	
Period	001	

Receiver Object	Sender object	Alloc. CElem	Ttl v. qty	TotFxdQty	TotF&Vqty	UoM	≡	TtlF+V/CAC	COCr	Template
ORD 60003992	BPR BP001	943100	0	0	0	EA		0.00	USD	MANUFACT
	ATY 1501/9010	943160	3.50	2.00	5.50	H		412.50	USD	MANUFACT
	ATY 1601/9020	943170	13.833	0.00	13.833	H		622.49	USD	MANUFACT
ORD 60003992 △							▪	1,034.99	USD	
△							▪▪	1,034.99	USD	

Figure 3.25: First allocation

No posting has occurred for business process BP001. BP001 is the standard pallet business process, which is selected because A-100 is not defined as a dangerous good. The actual allocation event defined in subtemplate WDGTPACK uses function OrderShipped, as shown in Figure 3.3. This returns no value at this point because the order status has not been set to DLV, which is the trigger for performing the allocation. No quantities are posted.

Cost center 1501/activity type 9010 is used to represent the initial setup time and the recalibration times. The fixed quantity of 2 H comes from the Actual Allocation Fixed formula in template MANUFACT (see Figure 3.2, ACTUAL FIX column). The variable quantity is derived from a formula that looks at total confirmed production (800) plus total reported scrap (30). 100 is subtracted from that to account for the initial setup procedure (see Figure 3.20). OrderYieldConfirmed represents the "good" production and OrderHeaderScrapQtyConfirm returns the scrapped amount. 830 minus 100 gives 730. This is then divided by 100 (7.3) and the integer portion of the number is used for the allocation (Floor function). Each recalibration takes a half hour, and 7 multiplied by 0.5 gives 3.5 hours. This appears in the variable column. A total of 5.5 hours is allocated for setup and recalibration time at this point.

Cost center 1601 and activity type 9020 represent the quality inspection time for each of the components. This also has to be performed for both good and scrapped production and so the allocation uses 830 to calculate the inspection time. Figure 3.19 shows the formula that uses functions OrderYieldConfirmed and OrderHeaderScrapQtyConfirm to calculate the total confirmation quantity. The total component quantity is handled by the flexible function `TotalOfBomItems` to return the total BOM items planned for the order. This is divided by the value returned by `TotalOrderQuantity` to get the number of BOM components for every single EA. Multiplying this result by the total confirmed quantity determines the number of inspections to be performed. The inspection for non-dangerous goods components takes half a minute, so the result is divided by 120 to calculate the hours. There are two components per EA, so the resulting formula is 830 multiplied by 2, divided by 120, which equals 13.833 hours.

Second allocation for order 60003992

The final confirmation of the order is for 655 EA of good production and 30 EA of scrap. The order status is now changed to CNF (see Figure 3.26). No more confirmations are expected, but no A-100 widgets have been reported into inventory.

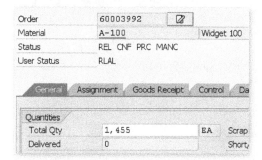

Figure 3.26: Order with final confirmation

Transaction CPTA is run again with the result showing in Figure 3.27. Now, 1,455 good EA and 60 scrapped EA have been confirmed.

Selection

Order	60003992	Widget 100
Version	0	Plan/Act - Version
Fiscal Year	2018	
Period	001	

Receiver Object	Sender object	Alloc. CElem	Tt v. qty	TotFxdQty	TotF&Vqty	UoM	TtF+V/CAC	COCr	Template
ORD 60003992	BPR BP001	943100	0	0	0	EA	0.00	USD	MANUFACT
	ATY 1501/9010	943160	7.00	2.00	9.00	H	675.00	USD	MANUFACT
	ATY 1601/9020	943170	25.25	0.00	25.25	H	1,136.25	USD	MANUFACT
ORD 60003992							1,811.25	USD	

Figure 3.27: Allocation after final confirmation of order

The resulting report from CPTA shows the total allocation that has occurred, including the result of the previous allocation. The DLV status has not yet been set, so there is still no allocation of business process BP001. The fixed value for activity type 1501/9010 is still 2, and has not changed. The actual fixed quantity is only allocated once, regardless of how many allocations there have been. The variable quantity has changed and reflects the total confirmed amount of 1,515 EA, including scrap. 1,515 minus 100 gives 1,415. This divided by 100 is 14.15, and the integer portion is 14. 14 recalibrations multiplied by 0.5 H gives 7 H associated with the variable portion of the allocation. The quality inspection formula also uses 1,515 and multiplies this by 2 to get 3,030 components to be inspected. This is divided by 120 to give 25.25 H of inspection time.

Third allocation for order 60003992

The final event for this order is the goods receipt of the 1,455 EA of A-100 to be shipped to the customer. This changes the order status to DLV (see Figure 3.28).

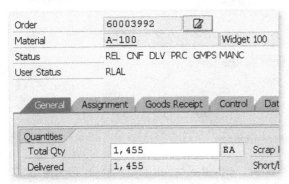

Figure 3.28: DLV status set for order

The CPTA allocation is now executed the results are posted, as shown in Figure 3.29. Note that the allocations for activity types 1501/9010 and 1601/9020 have not changed. There is now an allocation for business process BP001.

Selection

Order	60003992	Widget 100
Version	0	Plan/Act - Version
Fiscal Year	2018	
Period	001	

Receiver Object	Sender object	Alloc. CElem	Ttl v. qty	TotFxdQty	TotF&Vqty	UoM	⁞	TtlF+V/CAC	COCr	Template
ORD 60003992	BPR BP001	943100	25	0	25	EA		250.00	USD	MANUFACT
	ATY 1501/9010	943160	7.00	2.00	9.00	H		675.00	USD	MANUFACT
	ATY 1601/9020	943170	25.25	0.00	25.25	H		1,136.25	USD	MANUFACT
ORD 60003992 ⌂							⁙	2,061.25	USD	

Figure 3.29: Final allocation results

The BP001 allocation is performed because the Actual Allocation Event indicated that the period in which the DLV status was set (1) matched the period of the allocation run. The quantity calculation for this only uses the total quantity that was confirmed as good (OrderYieldConfirmed), because scrapped production does not get shipped. There are 60 EA per pallet (250 kg divided by 4.1 kg net weight per EA, rounded down to the nearest whole widget). 1,455 divided by 60 gives 24.25. Rounding this up to the nearest whole number using the Ceil function gives a result of 25.

The final results can be viewed in the order cost report (CO03 or KKBC_ORD). Figure 3.30 shows the actuals posted to the order.

Order	60003992 A-100
Order Type	PP01 Standard Production Order (int. number)
Plant	P100 Plant 100
Material	A-100 Widget 100
Planned Quantity	1,455 EA Each
Actual Quantity	1,455 EA Each

Transaction	Origin	Origin (Text)	Plan qty	Target qty	Actual Qty	⁞
Miscellaneous	BP001	Standard Pallets	25	24.735	25	
Confirmations	1501/9010	Plant Support / Support Hours	8.50	8.548	9.00	
Confirmations	1601/9020	Plant QC / QC Hours	24.25	24.25	25.25	

Figure 3.30: Order actual cost report after allocation

The allocation transactions also provide a means for tracing what was triggered during the template allocation. Select TEMPLATE TRACE from the GoTo dropdown menu (see Figure 3.31).

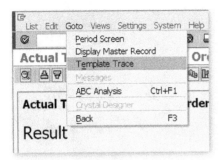

Figure 3.31: Template tracing menu

The system displays a representation of each of the lines of the template and any subtemplates, as shown in Figure 3.32. Open up a specific line to see the details. Looking at the Widget Packing line (subtemplate WDGTPACK), another set of items associated with that template is shown. The Standard Pallets line is then opened to see the results of each of the methods and formulas associated with the actual allocation that occurred.

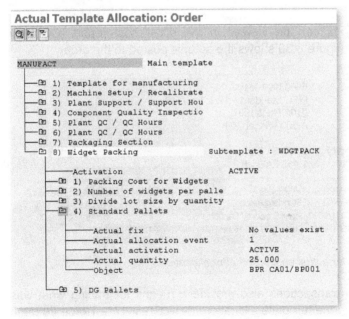

Figure 3.32: Template trace detail

4 Template configuration

SAP offers an extensive array of out-of-the-box functions and environments that are usually sufficient for use. Typically, there is very little configuration required beyond creating the template itself or defining how the template is connected to the cost object. However, template structures can be extended, and additional functions can be added to those structures, enhancing the template capabilities beyond what SAP delivers.

4.1 Template environments

Environments define the data and functions available for use by templates. The environments are set by SAP and are not able to be deleted. New environments cannot be created. Each environment is assigned to a Template Application which groups like environments together for maintenance purposes. A list of applications can be found in the appendix.

Environments are made up of one or more function trees, which in turn are made up of one or more structure nodes. Functions used for activation, object selection, and quantity formulas are assigned to the structure node. Although environments cannot be created or deleted, they can be extended by adding custom function trees and structure nodes. New functions can also be created and assigned to environments.

There are two types of environments. Main environments can be accessed when creating a specific template. There are also *sub-environments*, which contain a specific set of functions that operate on a common source of data such as materials or routes. Sub-environments cannot be directly associated with a template, but are instead assigned to one or more main environments. A main environment then has access to the functions in each sub-environment that is assigned to it. The delivered main environments do not directly access functions, but instead are connected via the sub-environment level. Sub-environments can be assigned to multiple main environments, and when a new function is added to a sub-environment, that function is automatically assigned to each main environment using the sub-environment.

There is a hierarchy associated with each environment or sub-environment. This hierarchy consists of *function trees*, *structure nodes*, and *function references*. The function tree denotes the first level under the environment. Function references can be assigned directly to the function tree, but they are normally assigned to the next level down in the hierarchy, called the structure node. The structure node level can be further sub-divided by assigning lower level structure nodes. The function reference is the link between the environment hierarchy and the function itself. When editing the template, the function is accessed in the formula or method using the function reference.

Basic environment configuration is done using transaction CTU6 or the IMG menu option: CONTROLLING • ACTIVITY-BASED COSTING • TEMPLATES • DEFINE ENVIRONMENTS AND FUNCTION TREES. Because templates are used in multiple areas of CO, this transaction can also be found under other sections of the CONTROLLING menu.

4.1.1 Working with environments

The first thing that is displayed when running CTU6 is a list of environments and sub-environments. These are identified with the 🗀 icon. There are two windows with information. The left window displays the environment hierarchy and the right window shows details of the object selected in the left window (see Figure 4.1). Function maintenance is performed in the right window.

Click on the 🢗 button to change which environments are displayed. Alternatively, choose the RESTRICT option from the FUNCTION TREE dropdown menu. Template Application, Environment, Function Tree, or a combination of the three can be chosen to limit the selections. Only those objects which match the filter criteria are displayed and can be edited.

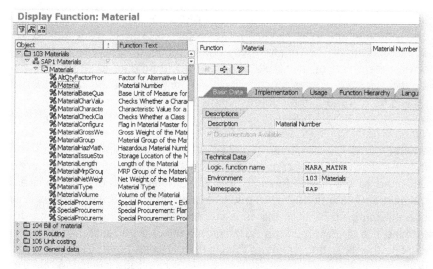

Figure 4.1: CTU6 windows

In order to view the function trees that belong to an environment, click on the ▷ button next to 🗀. A list of the function trees associated with that environment is displayed. Function trees are identified with the 🖧 icon. The list of structure nodes associated with each function tree can then be viewed by clicking on the ▷ button by the function tree. Opening the structure node level displays the list of functions or lower level nodes associated with that structure node. Clicking on ▽ at any level hides everything below that level.

No new environments can be created, nor can any environment be deleted. Configuration changes can only be made at the Function Tree level and below.

4.1.2   Sub-environments

A sub-environment is a structure that is used to group together functions that act on the same types of data. They are a special type of environment and have the same structure hierarchy as a standard environment. Templates can only be created for an environment and not for a sub-environment. Sub-environments are pre-assigned to regular environments and are usually assigned to more than one environment. New sub-environments cannot be created, and existing ones cannot be deleted. The functions and structure nodes of a sub-environment are available in all environments to which it is assigned. This is what makes the sub-environment so useful. Any new function created in a sub-environment can be available to all the environments to which it is assigned. Unless a new function is valid for a specific environment, it should be created at the sub-environment level.

When running transaction CTU6, the environments and sub-environments are displayed together, and distinguishing between them may be difficult. One factor to look at is the number of structure nodes assigned to the SAP1 function tree for that environment. If there are multiple structure nodes, then this is a main environment. If there is only one structure node, then this is a sub-environment. Another way to determine if a specific node is an environment or a sub-environment is to click on the ⣿ button or select the DISPLAY HIGHER-LEVEL ENVIRONMENTS option from the ENVIRONMENT dropdown menu. If the message "No selection possibilities exist" is displayed, this is a regular environment that can be used to create templates. If a list of environments is displayed, then this is a sub-environment, and the list shows all the environments to which it is assigned.

A list of sub-environments assigned to an environment is also available in CTU6. Click on the ⣿ button or select the DISPLAY LOWER-LEVEL ENVIRONMENTS option from the ENVIRONMENT dropdown menu. If only one environment is displayed, then no sub-environments are associated with it. Otherwise, the display includes the list of environments associated with it. Sub-environments do not show up in the hierarchy list. Instead, the structure nodes from the sub-environment are automatically associated with the function tree for that environment.

4.1.3 Function trees

Function trees are the structures used for organizing functions. Functions and structure nodes can be assigned to a function tree. The normal practice is to first assign a structure node to the tree and then assign the functions to the structure node. This helps to better organize the functions within a tree. Function trees have a four-character ID and a name, and they are assigned to a specific environment. Each environment is delivered with a special function tree using SAP1 as the ID. SAP1 function trees cannot be modified or deleted, but additional function references and structure nodes can be assigned to them. When maintaining templates, the function references used for specific cells are displayed using the active function tree structure for the environment.

Configuration options are found under the **Function Tree** drop down menu, as shown in Figure 4.2.

Figure 4.2: Function tree dropdown menu

Alternatively, select an environment or an existing function tree and click the right mouse button to see the menu of options for editing the function tree (see Figure 4.3). For custom function trees, all options are available. When clicking on the SAP1 function tree for an environment, then only REGENERATE FUNCTION TREE, COPY FUNCTION TREE, and (DE)ACTIVATE FUNCTION TREE are enabled for use. The CREATE FUNCTION TREE option can only be accessed by right-clicking on an environment.

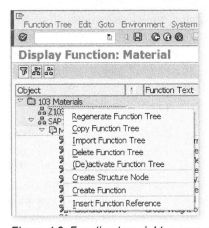

Figure 4.3: Function tree right mouse click menu

Create a function tree

Creating a function tree can be accomplished in one of two ways. First, select an environment by clicking on it. Then, hold down the right mouse button and select the CREATE FUNCTION TREE option. The other way to access function tree creation is to select an existing function tree in an environment and select the CREATE option from the FUNCTION TREE drop down menu. Enter an ID and a name for the new tree. It is assigned into the selected environment. Functions and structure nodes can now be added to this tree.

Recreate a function tree

The recreate option is used to reload the selected custom function tree with the delivered SAP1 function tree. This overwrites any structure that is already in place for that function tree. Select the function tree to be recreated and choose RECREATE from the FUNCTION TREE dropdown menu or press the right button on the mouse and choose the REGENER-ATE FUNCTION TREE option. The SAP1 function tree structure for that environment is assigned to the custom function tree. The recreate option can also be performed on the SAP1 function tree and can be used to correct any anomalies that may have occurred during customization.

Copy a function tree

Function trees can be copied within the same environment. A custom function tree can then be created containing the same tree structure and functions. When creating a new tree, it should be copied from the delivered SAP1 tree to ensure that all functions are available for the new tree. Changes can then be made to the new tree without affecting the original function tree. Activating the new tree makes those functions available for the environment. The previously active tree is then deactivated.

To copy a function tree, first select that tree by clicking on it. Then either choose the COPY option from the FUNCTION TREE menu or press the right mouse button and choose the COPY FUNCTION TREE option. Enter the new tree ID and name, and press [Enter]. The tree is then copied along with all structure nodes and function reference assignments under that tree.

Import a function tree

The Import option enables a function tree from another client to be imported into a function tree on the current client. This is not possible with a pre-delivered SAP1 function tree. Importing overwrites the tree on the current client. Select a non-SAP1 function tree and then either choose the IMPORT option from the FUNCTION TREE menu or press the right mouse button and choose the IMPORT FUNCTION TREE option. The system displays a window asking for a function tree, environment, and source client. The source client must be on the list of clients for the same system ID. Make the desired selections and press [Enter].

Activate/deactivate a function tree

Only one function tree can be active for an environment. By default, the SAP1 tree is active. If no other custom function tree defined for the environment is active, then the SAP1 tree is used, whether or not it has been explicitly made active. Once a custom function tree has been created, the functions assigned to this tree can only be used in a template if the tree is activated. The ▯ column contains a checkbox when the function tree is activated.

To activate a function tree, select an inactive function tree by clicking on it. Then, select (DE)ACTIVATE from the FUNCTION TREE dropdown menu or press the right button on the mouse and select (DE)ACTIVATE FUNCTION TREE from the menu. The function tree becomes active and a checkmark is displayed in the ▯ column. The previously active function tree is deactivated and the checkmark is removed from the ▯ column. Deactivating an active tree follows the same procedure. Select the active tree and follow the above instructions. The selected tree becomes inactive and the activation checkmark is assigned to the SAP1 function tree.

After saving the new configuration and exiting transaction CTU6, the function references assigned to the newly active tree are visible in templates for that environment. However, when reentering CTU6, it appears as though the SAP1 environment is activated. This is not the case. In order to activate the SAP1 tree again, first activate the custom tree and then activate the SAP1 tree.

Although custom function trees can be created for sub-environments, these cannot be accessed by the environments to which the sub-environments are assigned. This is due to the way that sub-environments are related to environments. Any function references that are created in the sub-environment custom trees are also created in the SAP1 tree.

Delete a function tree

A custom function tree and its entire structure can be removed by using the DELETE option. If the tree is active, the activation flag is reassigned to the SAP1 function tree for that environment. Select the function tree to be deleted and then choose the DELETE option from the FUNCTION TREE dropdown menu, or press the right mouse button and select the DELETE FUNCTION TREE option from the menu. The function tree and all its components are then deleted.

4.1.4 Structure nodes

Structure nodes are designated with the 🗩 icon. They are used to further group together functions under function trees. Grouping at this level makes it easier to select the proper function when creating templates. Structure nodes may be assigned to a function tree or another structure node, depending on the requirements of function grouping.

Each structure node defined for the SAP1 function tree of a main environment corresponds to the one structure node assigned to the SAP1 function tree of a sub-environment. This structure is pre-defined by SAP.

Structure nodes are maintained from the EDIT dropdown menu (see Figure 4.4). Select the STRUCTURE NODES option and then the desired maintenance option.

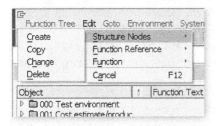

Figure 4.4: Structure node dropdown menu

Create a structure node

Structure nodes can be created by first selecting either a function tree or another structure node. The function tree cannot be one of the SAP-delivered SAP1 trees, and the structure node selected cannot be one of the structure nodes associated with an SAP1 function tree. SAP prevents any structure changes to the delivered function trees.

There are two ways for creating a structure node from the function tree level. First, right-click on the function tree under which the structure node belongs. Select CREATE STRUCTURE NODE from the menu. The other way is to select a function tree and select CREATE from the EDIT • STRUCTURE NODES dropdown menu. The system then asks for a name for the structure node.

When creating a structure node at the structure node level, first select the structure node by clicking the mouse on it. Either press the right mouse button and choose the CREATE STRUCTURE NODE option from the menu or go to the EDIT • STRUCTURE NODES dropdown menu and select CREATE. A window then appears for defining the structure node name. Additionally, there is a radio button selection for SAME LEVEL or LOWER LEVEL. Depending on which option is selected, the new node is placed either at the same level as the selected structure node, or in the hierarchy under that node.

Copy a structure node

Copying a structure node can be performed by using either the dropdown menus or the drag-and-drop method. Note that these two methods give different results. Using the dropdown menu, only the structure node is copied. Drag-and-drop, on the other hand, copies the entire structure.

For the dropdown menu method, first select the structure node to be copied. Then, either right-click the mouse on the structure and select COPY STRUCTURE NODE from the menu, or select COPY from the EDIT • STRUCTURE NODES dropdown menu. The SAME LEVEL and LOWER LEVEL selections are made available for placing the copied node. The copied structure node is then placed accordingly. The name cannot be changed at this point. To rename the copied structure nodes, you need to use the CHANGE function.

Copying via the dropdown menu method is limited because copied nodes can only be assigned in the same structure hierarchy. Using the drag-and-drop method enables a copied structure node to be assigned to a completely different hierarchy structure. With the left mouse button, click on the structure node to be copied. While still holding down the left button, drag the structure node to the new place in the hierarchy. The structure node, and all its components, is then copied to that new location. Of course, structure nodes cannot be copied into SAP1 function trees.

Change a structure node

The only thing that can be changed for a structure node is the name. This is useful so you can assign a new name to the copied structure node, thereby preventing confusion with duplicate names. First, select the structure node to be changed. Then, either right-click the mouse on the structure and select CHANGE STRUCTURE NODES from the menu, or select CHANGE from the EDIT • STRUCTURE NODES dropdown menu. The SAME LEVEL and LOWER LEVEL selections are then displayed, as per the Copy function, but these have no effect on the change. Make the necessary name changes and press Enter .

Delete a structure node

Structure nodes that are no longer needed can be deleted by selecting the structure node and using either the DELETE option of the EDIT • STRUCTURE NODES dropdown menu, or by using the right mouse button and selecting DELETE STRUCTURE NODE from the menu. The entire structure of the node is then removed.

4.1.5 Function references

A function reference is the object that points to a function. It is identified by the ⅙ icon. Function references can be assigned at the structure node level, or at the function tree level in the hierarchy. The reference is what is displayed in the template when selecting a function to use. When a new function is created, the corresponding function reference is also created. The function reference maintenance options can be found under the EDIT dropdown menu (see Figure 4.5), or from the menu retrieved by selecting a function reference and pressing the right button on the mouse.

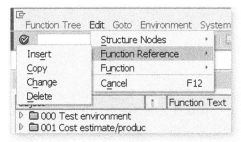

Figure 4.5: Function reference dropdown menu

Insert a function reference

A function reference defined in an environment can only be associated with a function that is also assigned to the same environment. When inserting a new function reference, first select either a function tree, or select a structure node under a function tree. New function references can be added to one of the delivered SAP1 trees as well as to a custom tree. Next, choose the INSERT option from the EDIT • FUNCTION REFER-ENCES dropdown menu or press the right mouse button and select the INSERT FUNCTION REFERENCE from the resulting menu. A window is displayed showing the available functions for the current environment. Select a function from the list. Another window is displayed with the selected function. If a function tree was originally selected, then the new function reference is added under that function reference. If a structure node was selected, then select either the SAME LEVEL or LOWER LEVEL radio button in the window. With SAME LEVEL, the function reference is added at the same level as the structure node. With LOWER LEVEL, the function reference is added under the selected structure node.

Copy a function reference

Function references can be copied within a function tree or a structure node setting. The copy is identical to the original. Select a function reference to copy. Choose the COPY option from the EDIT • FUNCTION REFERENCES dropdown menu or press the right mouse button and select the COPY FUNCTION REFERENCE option from the menu. Press ⌐Enter¬ to copy the function reference.

Change a function reference

When a function reference is changed, it points to a different function and takes on the name of the new function. Choose the CHANGE option from the EDIT • FUNCTION REFERENCE dropdown menu or press the right mouse button and select the CHANGE FUNCTION REFERENCE option from the menu. A window then displays all valid functions for the environment. Select the new function from the list and press ⌐Enter¬. The function reference now points to the selected function.

Delete a function reference

When a function reference is deleted, the reference is removed from the structure node or function tree, but the function itself is not affected. Function references cannot be deleted from SAP1 function trees. Select the function reference by clicking on it with the mouse and using either the DELETE option from the EDIT • FUNCTION REFERENCES dropdown menu or pressing the right button on the mouse and selecting DELETE FUNCTION REFERENCE from the menu. The reference is deleted from the function tree.

4.2 Template functions

The SAP-delivered set of functions might not satisfy all logic requirements for a specific implementation. There are two different types of functions that templates can use. The first is a Field Reference function. This returns the value of a specific field from a table. The table must be one of the tables accessible to the environment. The second type of function is an ABAP Reference function. These types of functions have parameters which are used in the determination of the values. New custom functions can be created which make use of parameters available in the environment.

The example used for demonstrating function maintenance is a Field Reference function. This type of function does not require the assistance of an ABAP programmer and is easy to configure.

New function for returning dangerous goods profile

 A template used in product costing needs to have access to the dangerous goods profile for a material. After searching through the list of functions currently available, no function can be found to return the value of this field. The dangerous goods profile is found in field PROFL in table MARA. A review of the tables available to the cost estimate environment and its sub-environments determines that MARA is a table that can be accessed for this purpose.

Functions can either be created from scratch or copied from an existing function.

The function maintenance menu can be found under the EDIT • FUNCTIONS dropdown menu, as shown in Figure 4.6.

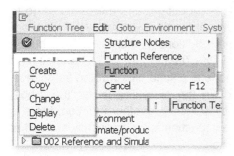

Figure 4.6: Function dropdown menu

First, a hierarchy component, such as a function tree, structure node, or function reference must be selected by clicking on it. Depending on the hierarchy level selected, certain maintenance options are not available. Function maintenance options are also available by right-clicking on the mouse when selecting the hierarchy object. The maintenance options available depend on which object is selected.

4.2.1 Create a Field Reference function

Functions are created from the function tree, structure node, or function reference level of the hierarchy. New functions can be added to the delivered SAP1 function structures, as well as to custom function trees.

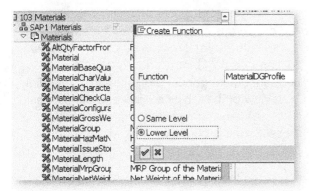

Figure 4.7: Create function window

When creating a function at the structure node level, first select the structure node by clicking the mouse on it. Either press the right mouse button and choose the CREATE FUNCTION option from the menu or go to the EDIT • FUNCTION dropdown menu and select CREATE. A window appears for defining the function name. Additionally, there is a radio button selection for SAME LEVEL or LOWER LEVEL (see Figure 4.7). Depending on which option is selected, the new node is placed either at the same level as the selected structure node, or in the hierarchy under that node. When the new function is created by selecting another function, there is no option to select the level. The new function is automatically created at the same level as the selected function.

Basic Data tab

In the BASIC DATA tab, enter a name for the function, as displayed in Figure 4.8. The LOGICAL FUNCTION NAME for a Field Reference function should include the name of the table and the name of the field, separated by an underscore. The field name for `MaterialDGProfile` is `PROFL`, from table `MARA`. The environment defaults to the current environment. The namespace field is optional and is used to prevent name clashes.

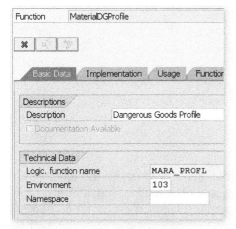

Figure 4.8: Function Basic Data tab

Namespaces are SAP-assigned identifiers which enable SAP customers, SAP partners and SAP itself to develop SAP components and products for applications without the risk of name clashes. Objects in the ABAP Workbench are assigned to a namespace by placing the reserved namespace prefix in front of the object name. The namespace identifier begins and ends with a "/" (delimiter) and can be maximum 10 characters long. Using a namespace requires a development license key. The namespace is not required and can be left blank for Field Reference functions because the logical function name references the table and field.

Implementation tab for Field Reference functions

Click on the IMPLEMENTATION tab to define the details of the function. Figure 4.9 shows the information required for a Field Reference function. Table name and field name are required. There is no need to make any changes in the FUNCTION REFERENCE section. The function returns the value of the field specified.

105

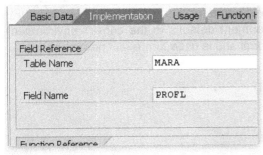

Figure 4.9: Implementation tab for field reference functions

Usage tab

The USAGE tab defines in which columns of a template the function applies. Functions can be used for quantity calculation, row activation, object determination, and event allocation. A function might not be applicable to one or more of these types of columns. To make sure that the new function can only be selected for columns which are able to use the result, click in the checkbox for each row and column type that is applicable. The OVERVIEW sub-tab, shown in Figure 4.10, is used for making the selections. `MaterialDGProfile` is used for activation but cannot be used for object determination, quantity calculations, event allocation, or in the determination of a complex condition for a flexible function.

Row Type	Object		Quantity		Activation		Allocation Event	
Business Process	☐	▽	☐	▽	☑	▽	☐	▽
Cost Center/Activity Type	☐	▽	☐	▽	☑	▽	☐	▽
Calculation Row (Business Process)	☐	▽	☐	▽	☑	▽	☐	▽
Calculation Row(Cost Center/Activity Type)	☐	▽	☐	▽	☑	▽	☐	▽
Flexible Function	☐	▽	☐	▽	☐	▽	☐	▽

Template Application: Cost objects

Tabs: Basic Data, Implementation, Usage, Function Hierarchy, Language

Sub-tabs: Overview, All Columns

Figure 4.10: Usage tab—Overview sub-tab

The TEMPLATE APPLICATION dropdown menu is important because the sub-environment could be associated with environments in multiple applications. Because row and column structure can differ between applications, it is important to make sure that the usage is updated in each application. Select the next application from the dropdown menu. Next, update the usage selections for that application (see Figure 4.11).

| Basic Data | Implementation | Usage | Function Hierarchy | Language |

Template Application: Easy Cost Planning

| Overview | All Columns |

Row Type	Object		Quantity		Activation	
Business Process	☐	▽	☐	▽	☑	▽
Cost Center/Activity Type	☐	▽	☐	▽	☑	▽
Calculation Row (Business Process)	☐	▽	☐	▽	☑	▽
Calculation Row(Cost Center/Activity Type)	☐	▽	☐	▽	☑	▽
Costing Model	☐	▽	☐	▽	☑	▽
External Activity	☐	▽	☐	▽	☑	▽
Subcontracting	☐	▽	☐	▽	☑	▽
Material	☐	▽	☐	▽	☑	▽
Service	☐	▽	☐	▽	☑	▽
Base Planning Object	☐	▽	☐	▽	☑	▽
Customer-Specific Enhancement	☐	▽	☐	▽	☑	▽
Text Item	☐	▽	☐	▽	☑	▽
Variable Item	☐	▽	☐	▽	☑	▽

Figure 4.11: Usage tab—Overview sub-tab for Easy Cost Planning

The ACTIVATION column in the OVERVIEW sub-tab refers to any type of activation, including both plan and actual activations. The new function might not be applicable to actual activation, but is only used for plan activation. This is controlled in the ALL COLUMNS sub-tab (see Figure 4.12).

| Overview | All Columns |

Row Type	Object		Quantity		Quantity plan fix		Activation plan		Quantity act		Quantity act		Activation
Business Pr.	☐	▽	☐	▽	☐	▽	☑	▽	☐	▽	☐	▽	☑
Cost Center.	☐	▽	☐	▽	☐	▽	☑	▽	☐	▽	☐	▽	☑
Calculation.	☐	▽	☐	▽	☐	▽	☑	▽	☐	▽	☐	▽	☑
Calculation.	☐	▽	☐	▽	☐	▽	☑	▽	☐	▽	☐	▽	☑
Flexible Fun.	☐	▽	☐	▽	☐	▽	☐	▽	☐	▽	☐	▽	☐

Figure 4.12: Usage tab—All Columns sub-tab

Function Hierarchy tab

The FUNCTION HIERARCHY tab shows the environments and sub-environments in which the function can be used. The appropriate standard SAP1 function trees are always selected and these cannot be changed. Changes are allowed for custom function trees and these can be selected or unselected depending on where the function should be assigned. Figure 4.13 shows the FUNCTION HIERARCHY tab information for this function.

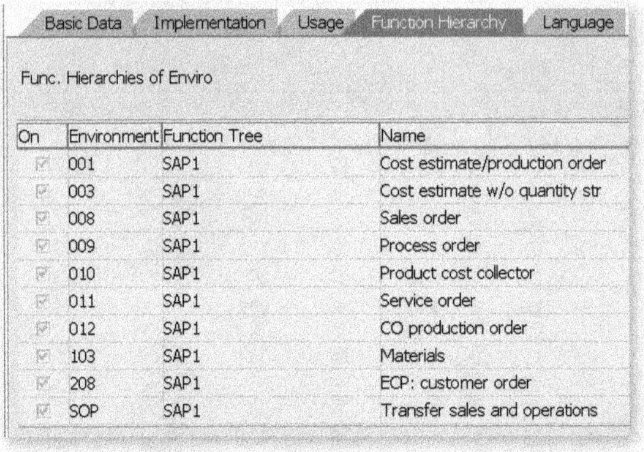

	Basic Data	Implementation	Usage	Function Hierarchy	Language

Func. Hierarchies of Enviro

On	Environment	Function Tree	Name
☑	001	SAP1	Cost estimate/production order
☑	003	SAP1	Cost estimate w/o quantity str
☑	008	SAP1	Sales order
☑	009	SAP1	Process order
☑	010	SAP1	Product cost collector
☑	011	SAP1	Service order
☑	012	SAP1	CO production order
☑	103	SAP1	Materials
☑	208	SAP1	ECP: customer order
☑	SOP	SAP1	Transfer sales and operations

Figure 4.13: Function Hierarchy tab

Language tab

The LANGUAGE tab enables functions to be accessed in the local language. By default, a new function is created only in the logon language. The function can be assigned to additional languages in this tab. This becomes important if it is necessary to assign functions to templates that are maintained in the local language. Dangerous Goods Profile has been defined in English, German, and French as shown in Figure 4.14.

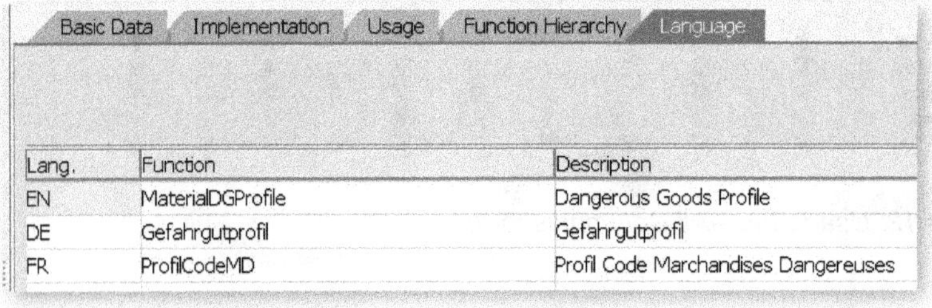

	Basic Data	Implementation	Usage	Function Hierarchy	Language

Lang.	Function	Description
EN	MaterialDGProfile	Dangerous Goods Profile
DE	Gefahrgutprofil	Gefahrgutprofil
FR	ProfilCodeMD	Profil Code Marchandises Dangereuses

Figure 4.14: Language tab

Saving the function

Once all the settings for the new function have been entered, the function must be saved. Click on the 💾 button. The new function shows up under the originally selected function tree. Functions that are created in a custom function tree for a sub-environment are also assigned to the SAP1 tree for that sub-environment. Functions that are created in a custom function tree for a main environment are only assigned to that custom function tree.

If the new function should not be saved, click on the ✖ button to cancel the creation of the function.

Function documentation

Documentation describing how a function works is maintained with the function. Function documentation can be viewed by selecting a function reference and selecting the FUNCTION DOCUMENTATION option of the GO-TO drop down menu or by press the right button on the mouse and selecting FUNCTION DOCUMENTATION from the menu. The system displays a description of the function, assuming one was created. Figure 4.15 shows documentation for a new field reference function returning the costing lot size.

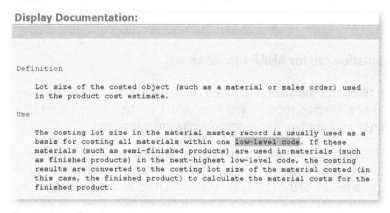

Figure 4.15: Function documentation

Click on the ✍ button on the BASIC DATA tab to create documentation for a new function. A window is displayed to select the language if the documentation is to be written in a language other than the login language. The system then brings up a word processor. Enter the text for the documentation and the save the changes. Return to the BASIC DATA tab using the ↩ button.

4.2.2   Create an ABAP Reference function

ABAP Reference functions access ABAP function modules, which can greatly extend both the logic available to the template and also the extent of data that can be accessed. For example, the template function `MaterialCharacteristicValue` accesses the material characteristics table, which is not readily available within environment 103. Returning a characteristic value also requires special logic to select the proper characteristic and return the value in the correct format.

Creating an ABAP Reference function is similar to creating a Field Reference function. The tabs for BASIC DATA, USAGE, FUNCTION HIERARCHY, and LANGUAGE are maintained in the same way. The differences begin when defining the IMPLEMENTATION tab. If the IMPLEMENTATION tab indicates that the function is an ABAP function, then a new PARAMETERS tab is enabled in order to define the parameters to be passed to the function module.

Implementation tab for ABAP functions

Figure 4.16 shows the values required for the IMPLEMENTATION tab. Enter the name of a function module and then select the type of result returned by the function. Four types of function types are supported:

▶ TRUE/FALSE—these functions return a Boolean value that is either a "true" value, indicating that the conditions specified by the parameters of the function have been met, or a "false" value, indicating that the conditions have not been met. These functions are used for activation methods.

▶ NUMB. VALUE/STRING—these functions return either a value that can be used in formulas or a string that can be used in activation or object determination.

▶ TYPE FROM PARAM.—these functions are used to identify an object, such as a business process or cost center/activity type. The type of the object is determined from the parameter that is assigned to the function when used in the template. The specific parameter to use is entered in the field next to the radio button selection. The parameter that is entered must be defined on the PARAMETERS tab. When this function is used in a template, the system checks to see if the result of the function can be used for the object type. If the types don't match, then a syntax error is declared.

▶ TYPE FROM FUNCTION—these functions are used to identify an object, such as a business process or cost center/activity type. These functions act similarly to the Type from Parameter functions, but the template function assigned in the field next to the radio button selection determines the type of result. For example, the function SenderProcess indicates a type associated with business processes.

A function can be declared as a flexible function by specifying the table/structure to be searched in the FLEX. FUNCTION VIA field. There are three possible tables: RESBD (Object List) for bills of materials, AFVGD (Routing), and KIS1 (Costing Items from Unit Costing). See Section 4.3 for information about flexible functions.

The REFERENCE FUNCTION entry is used when defining a function by copying an existing function and then modifying it to fit the new requirements. The new function refers to the existing function defined here.

POSSIBLE ENTRIES is used to identify the type of data that can be displayed when pressing ⎡F4⎤ for help. This is used when selecting parameters for ABAP functions and for selecting objects.

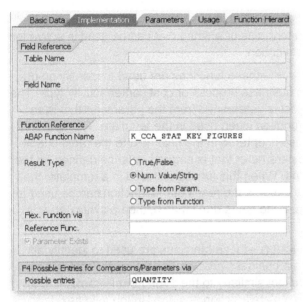

Figure 4.16: Implementation tab for ABAP functions

Parameters tab

The PARAMETERS tab is only visible when working with ABAP functions. This is where the parameters required by the function are defined. Figure 4.17 shows a listing of parameters assigned to the ABAP function K_CCA_STAT_KEY_FIGURES. All parameters that are required for the function to work must be defined here.

ABAP Parameter	Parameter	Typ	Default	Possbl	F4 Function Mo	Explanation
CALC_TYPE	CALC_TYPE	O	'1'			
FIELDGROUP	FieldGroup	I	'SME'			Field Group
GJAHR	FiscalYear	O	CurrentFiscalYear			Fiscal Year
KOKRS	ControllingArea	I	TemplateControllingArea			Controlling Area
KOSTL	CostCenter			KOSTL		Cost Center
LSTAR	ActivityType	O	''			Activity Type
PRZNR	Process	I	''			Process
STAGR	StatisticalKeyFigure					Statistical Key Figure
VERSN	Version	O	ActualVersion			Version
WRTTP	ValueType	I	'4'			Value Type

Figure 4.17: Parameters tab for ABAP functions

112

The parameters on this tab are imported from the function module that was specified on the IMPLEMENTATION tab. This includes the language dependent parameter names and the explanation. ABAP function modules are not specific to a template function. A single ABAP module can show up in several different template functions with different purposes. Defaults assigned to parameters affect the behavior of the ABAP function. Values in all columns except the ABAP PARAMETER column can be changed, but be careful of the resulting impact. The following list covers the information that is used for defining the parameters for the function module:

▶ ABAP PARAMETER—this is the parameter specified by the function module.

▶ PARAMETER—this is the name used in template maintenance for the ABAP parameter. This name belongs with a specific ABAP parameter, and if it is changed for one function, it then changes for all functions that use that parameter. Click on the LANGUAGE PARAM. button to change the name and description in languages other than the login language.

▶ TYPE—there are four different types that are allowed:

   ▶ Blank—when selecting the function for use in a template, the parameter does not have an assigned value. The value is required and must be assigned when adding the function to a formula or method.

   ▶ I—this is a hidden or invisible parameter. It is required by the function module, and a value must be assigned in the Default column. When using the function in a template, hidden parameters do not appear in the parameter list.

   ▶ L—this is a literal field that refers to a field name to be used in the module. This is used by the ABAP function to refer to a specific structure field. When assigning a value to one of these parameters, the format should be TABLE-FIELD (as in CBPRF-PRZNR for business process ID).

   ▶ O—this is an optional parameter. The ABAP function module has a default value assigned to this parameter if no value is entered during template maintenance.

▶ DEFAULT—this is the default value for the parameter. The default can either be a text item enclosed in single quotation marks or a reference to a template function to return the value. A list of available template functions is found in the dropdown list.

▶ POSSIBLE ENTRIES—this defines a data element which is used when pressing [F4] to determine what objects to list in the help selection window. In the example in Figure 4.17, KOSTL for the Cost Center row indicates that cost centers will be listed for selection when pressing [F4].

▶ F4 FUNCTION MODULE—this is a special ABAP function module that is called up when [F4] is pressed.

▶ EXPLANATION—this is the description associated with the parameter ID. This is also language dependent and can be maintained in alternative languages by clicking on the LANGUAGE PARAM. button.

Figure 4.18 shows the header for the corresponding ABAP function module detailing the defined parameters.

```
 1   FUNCTION k_cca_stat_key_figures.
 2   *"----------------------------------------------------------------------
 3   *"*"Lokale Schnittstelle:
 4   *"  IMPORTING
 5   *"     VALUE(KOKRS) LIKE  CCSS-KOKRS
 6   *"     VALUE(KOSTL) LIKE  CCSS-KOSTL
 7   *"     VALUE(LSTAR) LIKE  CCSS-LSTAR
 8   *"     VALUE(GJAHR) LIKE  CCSS-GJAHR
 9   *"     VALUE(WRTTP) LIKE  CCSS-WRTTP
10   *"     VALUE(VERSN) LIKE  CCSS-VERSN
11   *"     VALUE(STAGR) LIKE  CCSS-STAGR
12   *"     VALUE(CALC_TYPE) LIKE  ABC_F4_STRUCTURE-CALC_TYPE DEFAULT '1'
13   *"     VALUE(PERIOD_FROM)
14   *"     VALUE(PERIOD_CNT)
15   *"     VALUE(CALL_PROG) LIKE  SY-REPID
16   *"     VALUE(AUFNR) LIKE  AUFK-AUFNR OPTIONAL
17   *"     VALUE(PRZNR) LIKE  CCSS-PRZNR OPTIONAL
18   *"     VALUE(FIELDGROUP) DEFAULT 'SME'
19   *"  TABLES
20   *"     RTABLE_VAL TYPE  TPLIC_RVAL_TAB
21   *"----------------------------------------------------------------------
22       DATA: lt_cosra LIKE cosra OCCURS 0 WITH HEADER LINE.
```

Figure 4.18: ABAP function code

4.2.3 Copy a function

A good way to create a new function is to make a copy of an existing function. This can be done for both Field Reference functions and Function Reference (ABAP) functions. The copied function takes on the assignments and characteristics of the original function. A new Field Reference function can only be copied from an existing Field Reference function, and a new ABAP Function Reference function can only be copied from an existing ABAP Function Reference function.

Select the function to be copied by clicking on it. Choose the COPY option from the EDIT • FUNCTION dropdown menu or press the right mouse button and select COPY FUNCTION from the menu. Enter the name of the new function to be created (see Figure 4.19).

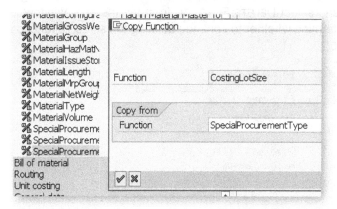

Figure 4.19: Copy function

Make the necessary changes and save the new function. Follow the instructions in Section 4.2.1 for making the changes.

4.2.4 Change a function

Select the function to be changed by clicking on it. Choose the CHANGE option from the EDIT • FUNCTION dropdown menu, or press the right mouse button and select CHANGE FUNCTION from the menu. Follow the instructions in Section 4.2.1 to change the function. Click on the 🖫 button to save the changes.

4.2.5 Display a function

Select the function to be displayed by clicking on it. Choose the DISPLAY option from the EDIT • FUNCTION dropdown menu or press the right mouse button and select DISPLAY FUNCTION from the menu. The selected function is then displayed in the right window. Click on the 🖉 button to switch to change mode. The 🖧 button is used to display a window with the list of templates in which the function is used.

4.2.6 Delete a function

Select the function to be displayed by clicking on it. Choose the DELETE option from the EDIT • FUNCTION dropdown menu or press the right mouse button and select DELETE FUNCTION from the menu. A window is displayed to determine whether to continue deleting the selected function (see Figure 4.20).

Figure 4.20: Delete custom function confirmation

If **Yes** is selected, the function and corresponding function reference is deleted from all function trees to which it is assigned. Click on the 🖫 button to complete the deletion.

SAP-delivered functions cannot be deleted. If this is attempted, the message shown in Figure 4.21 is displayed.

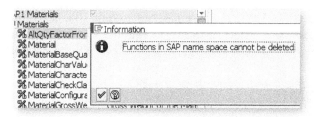

Figure 4.21: Attempt to delete SAP delivered function

4.3 Flexible functions

Chapters 2 and 3 used flexible functions in some of the quantity calculation cells in the MANUFACT template. Flexible functions are used in quantity calculations and to evaluate data in internal tables based on user-defined conditions. Instead of acting on a single field, these functions work with the fields of all the rows in an internal table. Internal tables for BOM components, routing operations, and unit costing items can be used with flexible functions. The delivered flexible functions provide three different calculations that are applied to the tables:

▶ Total—adds the values of the selected fields together and returns the total.

▶ Multiplication—multiplies the values of the selected fields together and returns the result.

▶ Average—returns the average of the values of the selected fields.

One ABAP module is used for the three different calculations and the calculation type is assigned as an invisible parameter to the ABAP function in CTU6. A flexible function consists of the following components:

▶ internal table containing the data to be evaluated

▶ condition to check for each table entry

▶ formula providing a value associated with the table entry

▶ calculation type, such as a total or average which is applied to the formula results for all table entries

Three flexible functions are delivered in sub-environment 104, which is used for bills of materials. TotalOfBomItems returns a value that is generated by adding the values returned from each of the individual BOM components. AverageOfBomItems returns a value that is the average of the values calculated for each of the BOM components. The final flexible function MultipleOfBomItems returns the values associated with each BOM item multiplied together.

To determine which BOM components are used for calculating the individual values, a condition is passed to the function. This condition is similar to a method that is used for activation. In this case, the activation determines whether the internal table row associated with the component is used in the overall calculation. Template functions that have been enabled for use in flexible functions for the environment can be used in the method. A formula is also created and is used to calculate the value for that particular row. Finally, the values calculated for each of the calculated rows are added together to return the ultimate value for the flexible function.

Calculating warehouse activity using a flexible function

 Capturing the amount of activity for moving BOM components from the warehouse to the manufacturing floor is dependent on the number of components on the BOM. The BOMs also contain text items for use in manufacturing paperwork. These BOM items should be excluded from the calculation of the activity quantity. It takes three minutes to move one of each component item to the floor. If there are two of the same components in the BOM, then it takes twice as long. There is also a fixed time of twelve minutes to process each order.

The example uses function TotalOfBomItems to add together the quantities of all the true BOM components to calculate the amount of warehouse activity to allocate. Select this from the list of functions in the right-hand window. Two things then happen. First, the function is assigned to the formula window, as shown in Figure 4.22.

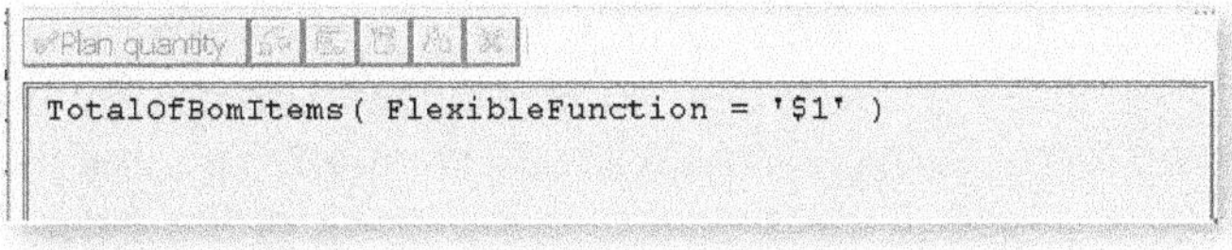

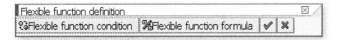

Figure 4.22: Flexible function in the formula window

Then, a separate window is displayed with buttons to create the method used for the selection condition. Click on the FLEXIBLE FUNCTION CONDITION button, as shown in Figure 4.23.

```
Flexible function definition                                    ⊠
😕Flexible function condition  %Flexible function formula  ✔  ✖
```

Figure 4.23: Flexible function condition and formula window

The main formula window now switches to enable the creation of the condition method (see Figure 4.24). The flexible function condition assigned to it looks at the value of the item category (field POSTP in structure RESBD) to determine if it is a warehouse component (L). Save the method by clicking on the FLEXIBLE FUNCTION CONDITION button for the formula window.

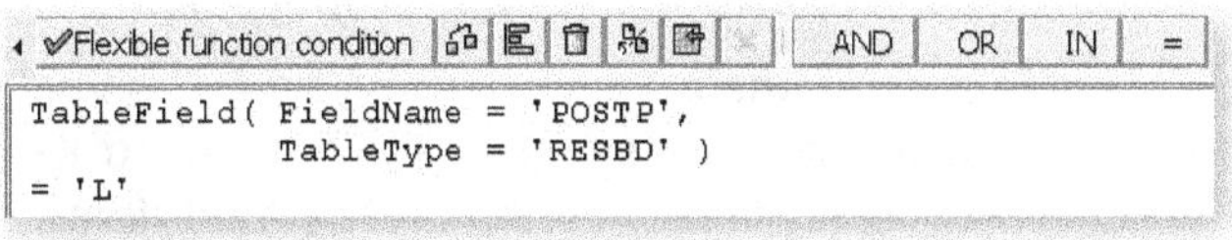

```
◄ ✔Flexible function condition  [icons]     AND   OR   IN   =
TableField( FieldName = 'POSTP',
            TableType = 'RESBD' )
= 'L'
```

Figure 4.24: Selection method for the flexible function

Next, click on the FLEXIBLE FUNCTION FORMULA button in the FLEXIBLE FUNCTION DEFINITION window (see Figure 4.23). The flexible function formula then looks at the quantity of each BOM component and divides that by the BOM base quantity, and then multiplies by 0.05 (one twentieth of an hour, or 3 minutes) to calculate the amount of warehouse activity for that BOM item. To save the formula, click on the FLEXIBLE FUNCTION FORMULA button, as shown in Figure 4.25.

```
✔Flexible function formula  [icons]     +   -   *   /   (   )
BomItemRequiredQuantity
/ OrderBomBaseQuantity
  * .05
```

Figure 4.25: Value calculation for each BOM item

After the selection condition and formula have been defined, click on the ✔ button in the FLEXIBLE FUNCTION DEFINITION window. The display returns to the PLAN QUANTITY formula window (see Figure 4.26) so that the rest of the formula is added. 0.20 is added to the result of the flexible function to calculate the total amount of activity type 9000 to be allocated to the cost.

Figure 4.26: The completed plan quantity formula

A BOM has the following information which is used for the flexible function to calculate the times:

- ▶ BOM base quantity is 100
- ▶ BOM item line 1: item category T, quantity 1
- ▶ BOM item line 2: item category L, quantity 500
- ▶ BOM item line 3: item category L, quantity 1,000
- ▶ BOM item line 4: item category L, quantity 300

In this case, `TotalOfBomItems` returns a value of 0.9. The first component item is ignored because the item category is T. The second item returns 0.25 (500 divided by 100 multiplied by 0.05). The third item returns 0.5 (1,000 divided by 100 multiplied by 0.05). The final item returns 0.15 (300 divided by 100 multiplied by 0.05). Because this is a "total" flexible function, these values are added together to give 0.9.

The average function `AverageOfBomItems` returns a value of 0.3 for the same condition and formula (0.9 divided by 3 components). The multiple function `MultipleOfBomItems` returns 0.01875 (0.25 multiplied by 0.5 multiplied by 0.15).

The same ABAP function is used for all three of these flexible functions. The type of calculation is an invisible parameter that is passed to the ABAP code.

Flexible functions are distinguished in the list of function references by using blue font instead of black. When creating a flexible function, the function needs to be assigned to the internal table made available for the purpose in the FLEX. FUNCTION VIA field (see Figure 4.27). The available structures are **Object List** (structure `RESBD`), **Routing** (structure `AFVGD`), and **Costing Items** from **Unit Costing** (structure `KIS1`).

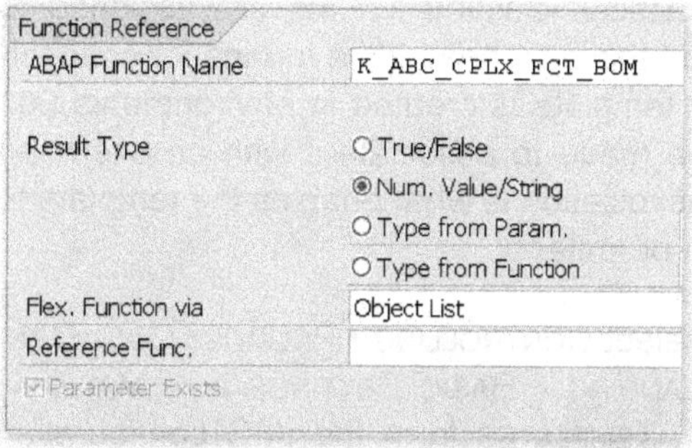

Function Reference	
ABAP Function Name	K_ABC_CPLX_FCT_BOM
Result Type	○ True/False
	◉ Num. Value/String
	○ Type from Param.
	○ Type from Function
Flex. Function via	Object List
Reference Func.	
☑ Parameter Exists	

Figure 4.27: Flexible function implementation tab definition

Parameters for a flexible function must include an aggregation type, which controls the type of output of the function. The supported values are 'A' for average, 'M' for multiplication, and 'S' for total. The function shown in Figure 4.28 is defined for generating a Total result (AGGRE-GATION_TYPE set to 'S').

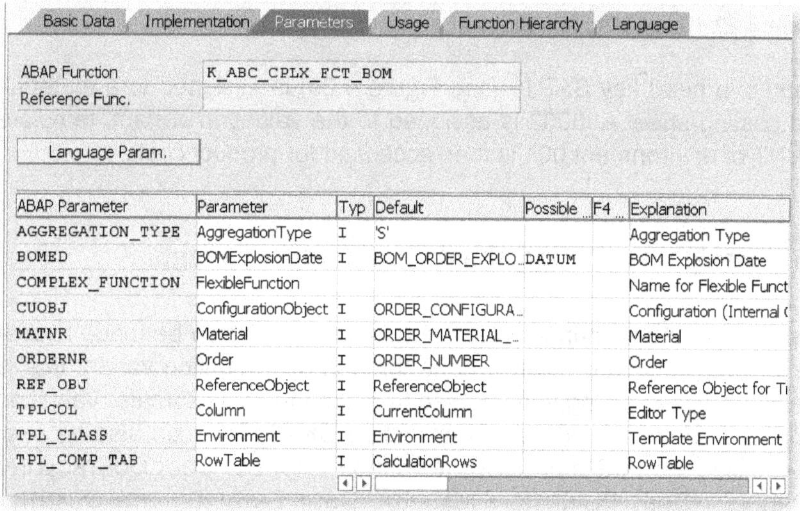

Basic Data	Implementation	Parameters	Usage	Function Hierarchy	Language

ABAP Function	K_ABC_CPLX_FCT_BOM
Reference Func.	

Language Param.

ABAP Parameter	Parameter	Typ	Default	Possible	F4	Explanation
AGGREGATION_TYPE	AggregationType	I	'S'			Aggregation Type
BOMED	BOMExplosionDate	I	BOM_ORDER_EXPLO..DATUM			BOM Explosion Date
COMPLEX_FUNCTION	FlexibleFunction					Name for Flexible Funct
CUOBJ	ConfigurationObject	I	ORDER_CONFIGURA..			Configuration (Internal (
MATNR	Material	I	ORDER_MATERIAL_..			Material
ORDERNR	Order	I	ORDER_NUMBER			Order
REF_OBJ	ReferenceObject	I	ReferenceObject			Reference Object for Ti
TPLCOL	Column	I	CurrentColumn			Editor Type
TPL_CLASS	Environment	I	Environment			Template Environment
TPL_COMP_TAB	RowTable	I	CalculationRows			RowTable

Figure 4.28: Flexible function parameters

121

4.4   Assigning templates to costing sheets

For most Controlling modules, the templates are assigned as a part of the master data of the receiving cost objects. When it comes to Product Cost Controlling, the receivers are either material cost estimates or manufacturing orders. The sheer numbers of these objects make specific assignment of templates impractical. Costing Sheets are assigned to materials via Overhead Key, and this also provides a means for connecting the template. When a new template is created in environments 001 to 012, an assignment must be made to associate it with an overhead key and a costing sheet. This association is what enables the template to be accessible to the cost object or material.

Execute transaction KTPF or select CONTROLLING • PRODUCT COST CONTROLLING • PRODUCT COST PLANNING • BASIC SETTINGS FOR MATERIAL COSTING • TEMPLATES • ASSIGN TEMPLATES from the IMG configuration menu. Click on the NEW ENTRIES button. The assignment uses controlling area, costing sheet, overhead key, environment, and template.

New Entries: Overview of Added Entries

COAr	CostSh	OH key	Environ.	Template	Name
CA01	A00002	SAP10	001	MAINT	

Figure 4.29: Connecting templates to a costing sheet

When overhead key SAP10 (see Figure 4.29) is assigned to a material, and costing sheet A00002 is assigned to the valuation variant, template MAINT of environment 001 is then accessed for product costs.

4.5   Assigning costing sheets to valuation variants

The costing sheet connected to the template must also be made available for cost estimates. This is done through the valuation variant that is assigned to the costing variant used to make the cost estimate. Valuation variants are maintained using transaction OKK4. This can also be executed using the IMG menu: CONTROLLING • PRODUCT COST CONTROLLING • PRODUCT COST PLANNING • MATERIAL COST ESTIMATE WITH QUANTITY STRUCTURE • COSTING VARIANT: COMPONENTS • DEFINE VALUATION VARI-

ANTS. Select the valuation variant to modify and then go to the OVERHEAD tab. Figure 4.30 shows where the costing sheet is assigned.

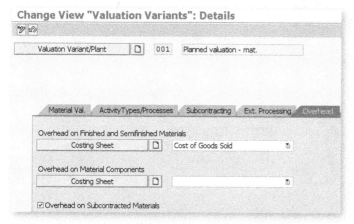

Figure 4.30: Overhead tab for valuation variant maintenance

Costing sheets can be used for cost estimates of manufactured and purchased materials. Enter the template for the appropriate type of material.

Plant-specific configuration

 Differences in calculation requirements for individual plants could make it difficult to be able to use one template for all plants. There are two ways to accommodate this. One way is to make a plant-specific valuation variant. Click on the VALUATION VARIANT/PLANT button (see Figure 4.30) to create a variant for a specific plant. Make any changes necessary for that specific plant. A template that pertains only to that plant can be assigned to the variant. The other way is to use subtemplates. A subtemplate can be a row object. Assign the plant specific template to that row and check for plant in the activation column.

123

5 Template applications

Chapters 2 and 3 looked in detail at templates used for plan and actual allocations in a single environment. Environments are assigned to applications, and nine different applications have been defined. Environment 001 is only one of twelve environments associated with the Cost Object application, and each application has one or more environments assigned to it. The scope of this book does not allow a detailed review of all applications and environments; this chapter introduces them and provides background information about how they are used, and which transactions enable template allocations to be processed.

5.1 Template applications

A template *application* is a grouping of environments that act on similar types of receiver objects for a common purpose. For example, environment 001 from application COB is used for plan and actual cost allocations for production orders and standard cost estimates. There are eleven other environments for COB, all of which involve allocations with different types of orders and cost estimates. A list of applications is shown in Table 7.1 in the appendix. The allowed row types for an environment are common to all environments within an application. This is found in Table 7.5 of the appendix. The column types available are environment specific and may differ for each of the environments assigned to an application. The column types for each environment can be viewed in Table 7.6.

5.2 COB—cost objects

COB application templates are used in allocations for cost objects associated with orders and projects. Most cost objects support both plan and actual allocations. The plan allocations are included in object cost estimates that use special costing variants. Some of the environments are also used in the creation of cost estimates for materials using quantity structures (environment 001), base planning objects (environment 002), materials without quantity structures (environment 003 for unit cost), and sales order line items with valued inventory (environment 008).

One common thread for this application's environments is that the cost objects are connected to the templates using overhead keys assigned to the specific cost object. Configuration is used to assign an overhead key to a costing sheet and template (see Figure 5.1). The costing sheet is then assigned to the valuation variant defined for the costing variant for the cost estimate in question. The details of this configuration are covered in Section 4.4. Up to three different cost estimates are associated with an environment. For example, environment 001 for production orders uses the standard cost estimate for a material, a preliminary plan cost estimate for the production order, and a cost estimate used for simultaneous or actual costing. For an allocation to occur, the overhead key must be defined for the specific receiver object. Then, based on the template assignment in configuration, the allocation takes place as a part of the generation of the cost estimate.

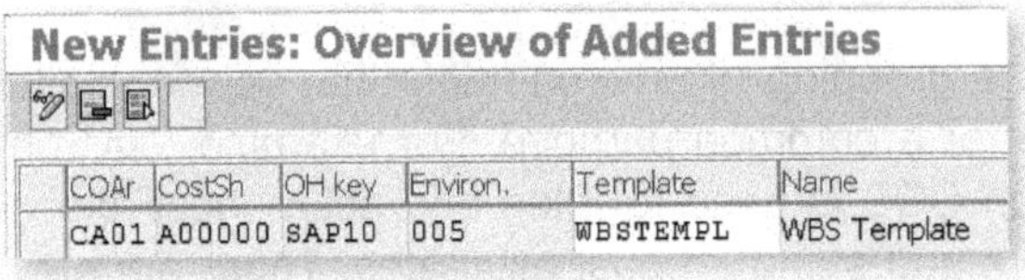

New Entries: Overview of Added Entries

COAr	CostSh	OH key	Environ.	Template	Name
CA01	A00000	SAP10	005	WBSTEMPL	WBS Template

Figure 5.1: Example of overhead key configuration with KTPF

5.2.1 Environment 001—production orders

This environment is used for standard cost estimates with quantity structure and production orders (order category 10). This was covered in detail in Chapters 2 and 3. Standard cost estimates use only plan allocations. Production orders create a plan cost estimate when the order is saved. Actual costs are posted as a part of normal order activity, which includes goods issues and production confirmations. However, the allocation of actual costs for overhead not associated with confirmations is only applied during period end closing. Template allocations are then made using either transaction CPTA for a single order or transaction CPTD for all orders in a plant. The overhead key is assigned in the material master. When an order is created, the overhead key is copied from the material into the order, and order allocations are made based on this overhead key assignment.

5.2.2 Environment 002—base planning objects

Base planning objects are manually built cost estimates that are not associated directly with a material. They exist as independent cost estimates that can be included in other types of costs, such as cost estimates without quantity structure or Easy Cost Planning costs. No actual costs are associated with base planning objects and the templates of this environment do not support actual allocations. Transaction KKE1 creates the base planning object (see Figure 5.2). The overhead key required to link the base planning object to the template is manually assigned at the header level. The second part of the link to the template is the costing sheet. If a costing sheet is assigned to the valuation variant used for base planning object costing, then that costing sheet is automatically used. Otherwise, enter a costing sheet so that the template is linked to the cost estimate.

Base Planning Object	NEW WIDGET	Controlling Area	CA01
General data			
Base Unit of Measure	EA	Cost Element	
Company Code	CC01	Base Object Group	
Plant	P100	Sort Field	
Profit Center			
Costing Sheet	A00000	Overhead key	WIDGET

Figure 5.2: Base planning object overhead key assignment

The allocation is made when the cost estimate is saved. To see the allocation prior to saving the cost estimate, select CALCULATE OVERHEAD from the FUNCTIONS dropdown menu. Item 2 on the cost estimate in Figure 5.4 was allocated using template BPOTEMPL in environment 002 (see Figure 5.3).

New Entries: Overview of Added Entries

COAr	CostSh	OH key	Environ.	Template	Name
CA01	A00000	WIDGET	002	BPOTEMPL	Base Planning Object Template

Figure 5.3: Configuration for connecting BPOTEMPL

127

		Item	C	Resource	Plant/Ac	Purc.	Quantity	Unit	L	Value - Total	Description

Base Planning Obj   NEW WIDGET   New Widget

Costing Items - Basic View

	M	Item	C	Resource	Plant/Ac	Purc	Quantity	Unit	L	Value - Total	Description
		1M	A-300	P100			1,000	EA		0.10	Widget 300
		2X	BP001				100	EA		1,000.00	Pack using standard pallets

Figure 5.4: Template allocation result

SAP intended that base planning objects would no longer be supported in S/4HANA. The recommendation was to replace this functionality by using transaction CKUC for unit cost estimates (environment 003) and CKECP from Easy Cost Planning (environment 200). Refer to SAP notes 1946054[1] and 2349294[2] for more details. However, even before release 1709, most of the base planning object functionality has been restored, including transactions KKE1, KKE2, and KKE3. Refer to SAP Note 2133644[3] for details.

5.2.3 Environment 003—unit cost estimates

Unit cost estimates (cost estimates without quantity structure) are created for a material when the BOM and routing information is not available. The costing variant normally used for these types of cost estimates is the same as for cost estimates with quantity structure. Since the costing variant is the same, the valuation variant is also the same, and this points to the same costing sheet as is used for the connection for environment 001 templates. Figure 5.5 shows that the same overhead key has been used as in the earlier examples. Since the environment is different, a different template can be assigned. Of course, other overhead keys and templates can be configured as well.

Change View "View for Template Determination": Ov

New Entries

COAr	CostSh	OH key	Environ.	Template	Name
CA01	COGS	WIDGET	003	UCTEMPL	Unit Cost Estimate Template

Figure 5.5: Configuration for connecting UCTEMPL

---

[1] Note 1946054 – SAP Simple Finance, on-premise edition: Transaction codes and programs – Comparison to EHP7 and EHP8 for SAP ERP 6.0

[2] Note 2349294 – S4TWL – Reference and Simulation Costing

[3] Note 2133644 – Error message SFIN_FI 004: Transactions KKE1, KKE2, KKE3 cannot be called

The costs are manually built for each costing item using transaction CKUC. When first viewing the window for adding the cost estimate items, the allocations from the template are displayed (see Figure 5.6).

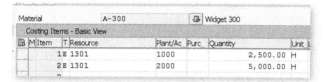

Figure 5.6: Allocation from template UCTEMPL

These allocations are based on the costing lot size, which is 10,000 for material A-300. Figure 5.7 shows the calculation for the allocation of activity type 1000 from cost center 1301.

Template	UCTEMPL	Unit Cost Estimate Template
Environment	003	Cost estimate w/o quantity str.

Template overview : display

Type	Description	Object	Unit	Plan quantity	Plan activation
Cost Center/Activity Type	Manufacturing	1301 / 1000	H	UnitCostingLot	MaterialDGPro
Cost Center/Activity Type	Manufacturing	1301 / 2000	H	UnitCostingLot	MaterialDGPro

Plan quantity   +   -   *   /   (   )

UnitCostingLotSize / 4	Functions for ▽ SAP1 Cc ▽ Send

Figure 5.7: Plan quantity for template UCTEMPL

Depending on how the template is defined, the allocation quantities may change after additional cost items have been added. To recalculate the allocation, select CALCULATE OVERHEAD from the FUNCTIONS dropdown menu (see Figure 5.8).

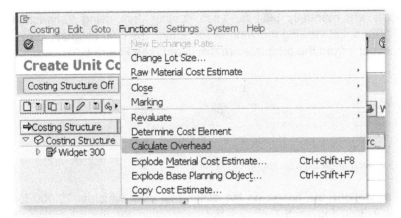

Figure 5.8 : Calculate overhead dropdown menu—CKUC

There are three flexible functions that are associated with unit cost estimate. These are found in sub-environment 106 and are available in some other environments that might encounter unit cost estimates. The unit costing flexible functions are `AverageCostingItems`, `MultipleCostingItems`, and `TotalCostingItems`. Since unit cost estimates do not have access to BOMs and task lists (routes or recipes), these flexible functions take the place of the corresponding ones for BOMs and routes that are accessible to other COB application environments.

5.2.4   Environment 004—networks

Both plan and actual template allocations can be performed for networks. The overhead key and costing sheet required to activate the template is on the CONTROL tab of the network definition. The COSTING section shown in Figure 5.9 shows the link to costing sheet A00000 and overhead key SAP10.

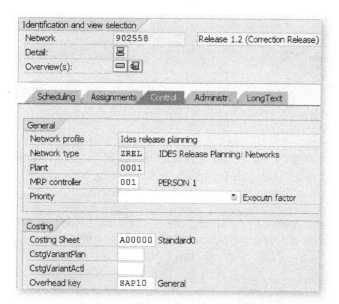

Figure 5.9: Network definition from the project builder (CJ20N)

Cost planning for projects can be performed at the network level and the WBS element level. Template allocations can be made as part of the planning process as well for actual costs. Unlike production orders, preliminary cost estimates are created manually when creating the network. No material cost estimate is involved, so plan allocations are not made as they are with other COB environments. Special plan allocation transactions are provided. Chapter 3 introduced the concept of an allocation event for actual allocation. The order event was the fiscal period when a specific status was set in the order, and controlled when the allocation would be processed. Due to the nature of cost planning for networks and WBS elements, these environments also contain a plan allocation event column for triggering plan allocations during the correct period. Special functions return the period for certain network events, as shown in Figure 5.10.

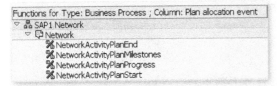

Figure 5.10: Environment 004 allocation event functions

Four functions are provided for plan allocation events and another four for actual allocation events. Each function returns the period of the time a specific event occurs. This can be used in addition to the activation method to determine whether to perform the specific allocation.

Four transactions are used for processing the allocations. CPUK is used for plan allocations for a single project or WBS element, including all the networks assigned to the WBS element (see Figure 5.11).

Plan Template Allocation: Project/WBS Element/Network

Project	X-IDES-2
or	
WBS Element	

☐ With hierarchy
☐ With orders

Parameters
Version	0	Plan/Act - Version
Period	1 To	12
Fiscal Year	2018	

Processing Options
☐ Background Processing
☑ Test Run
☑ Detail Lists

Figure 5.11: Template allocation with transaction CPUK

Transaction CPUL performs the plan allocation for multiple WBS elements and networks. The corresponding transactions for actual allocations are CPTK and CPTL.

5.2.5 Environment 005—WBS elements

Environment 005 is used for allocations to WBS elements. This works similarly to environment 004, and it also processes plan and actual allocations. The assignment of the costing sheet and overhead key to trigger the allocations is in the ACCOUNTING section of the CONTROL tab of the WBS element definition (see Figure 5.12).

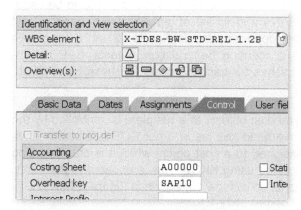

Figure 5.12: WBS element definition from the project builder (CJ20N)

Like network templates, WBS templates use allocation event methods for plan and actual allocations. Function WBSElementActualStart, shown in Figure 5.13, returns the period in which the Actual Start Date in the DATES tab of the WBS Element was set.

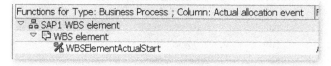

Figure 5.13 : Environment 005 allocation event functions

WBS plan allocations are performed by transactions CPUK and CPUL along with the network plan allocations of environment 004. The actual allocation transactions are CPTK and CPTL.

5.2.6   Environment 006—general cost objects

General cost objects do not fit into a standard category for orders and are used for tracking costs in the Intangible Goods and Services area of CO. General cost objects require the same types of planning and period end activities as for other cost objects, and environment 006 was created to cover plan and actual template allocations for these cost objects. General cost objects must be enabled for a controlling area to be used. With the arrival of S/4HANA and its list of simplifications, general cost objects will no longer be supported. See SAP note 2270411[4] for details about the simplification concerning general cost objects. SAP recommends alternative approaches for handling costs for these types of objects.

The connection of general cost objects to a template is controlled by the costing sheet and the overhead key, as in other COB application environments. These are assigned to a cost object when it is created using transaction KKC1 or modified using KKC2. This is updated in the COST-ING section of the maintenance window, as shown in Figure 5.14.

Cost Object	GENORDER		Cost obj. cat.
Short Text	General Order		
General Data			
Controlling Area	CA01		CO N. America
Company Code	CC01		IDES US INC
Business Area	9000		Accessories
Functional Area			
Plant	P100		Plant 100
Profit Center	10001		Widgets
Object Currency	USD		American Dollar
Person Responsible			
Costing			
Costing sheet	PP-PC1		PP-PC Standard
Overhead key	SAP10		

Figure 5.14: Template connection in KKC1

---

[4] Note 2270411 - S4TWL - General Cost Objects and Cost Object Hierarchies

The connection to a template for environment 006 is configured with transaction KTPF, as it is with the other cost objects. There are four transactions for template allocations. CPUA and CPUB are for plan allocations for single cost objects and multiple cost objects respectively. These transactions are also used for plan allocations for internal orders and only find general cost objects if they have been enabled for the controlling area. The two actual allocation transactions are CPTG for a single cost object and CPTH for multiple cost objects. See Figure 5.15 for an example of the allocation for a single order.

Actual Template Allocation: Cost Object

Cost Object	GENORDER	General Order
Parameters		
Version	0	Plan/Act - Version
Period	2 To	
Fiscal Year	2018	

Processing Options
☐ Background Processing
☑ Test Run
☑ Detail Lists

Figure 5.15: General cost object template allocation - CPTG

CPTG and CPTH are not available in S/4HANA, but CPUA and CPUB are still functional because they are also used for internal orders.

5.2.7 Environment 007—internal orders

Internal orders are objects that are used to group costs and revenues for specific internal jobs or tasks. Costs can be planned for internal orders, and these are compared to the actual costs that are posted to the order. Costs for internal orders are settled during period end closing activities. Template allocation for activity types and business processes can be used as part of the planning and period end closing functions.

Connecting a template to an internal order is done by assigning the costing sheet and overhead key using KO01 or KO02. The layout of internal order screens is highly customizable. Make sure these fields are available for use for the specific order type. Figure 5.16 shows the assignment of costing sheet and overhead key in the PERIOD-END CLOSING section of the PRD-END CLOSING tab.

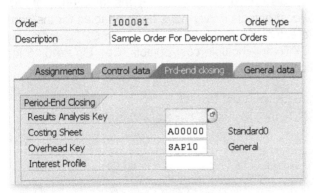

Figure 5.16: Template connection in KO01

Transactions CPUA and CPUB are used for processing plan allocations. CPUA is for single orders, and CPUB is for multiple orders. CPTA and CPTB are used for actual template allocations. Figure 5.17 shows the transaction for actual template allocation for multiple orders.

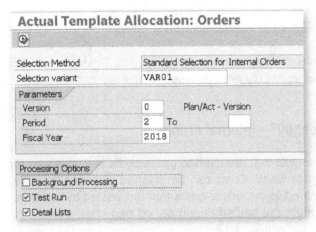

Figure 5.17: Actual template allocation for multiple internal orders

The transaction requires that a selection variant be defined to narrow the selection to orders of a certain order type or to those which have certain characteristics. CPUB and CPTB are used for allocations in multiple environments and the values defined in the variant help determine which environment are used in the allocation.

5.2.8   Environment 008—sales orders

This environment is used for both sales order cost estimates and for actual allocations to sales orders when the sales order line item is a cost object. Sales order cost estimates are generated in conjunction with the creation of sales orders and depend on the requirements class assigned to an order line item. Sales order cost estimates can be used for inventory valuation purposes if the sales order stock is valued. If the sales order stock is not valued, then the cost estimate is used as a planned cost for the order. In this case, the order line item is a cost object and the costs are settled directly to the sales orders. Cost estimates can be set up to be automatically created when the order is saved, or they can be created or recreated using transaction CK51N. Normally, valuation variant 001 is assigned to sales order cost estimate costing variants, and the link to the template through the costing sheet would be the same as for a standard cost estimate. The overhead key is transferred from the material, and that key must be included in the configuration in transaction KTPF.

Environment 008 templates are set up to use both plan and actual allocations. When using the sales order as a cost object, actual costs are settled to the sales order line item. Template allocation can occur for actual costs prior to settlement. Transaction CPTJ is used to process these allocations (see Figure 5.18).

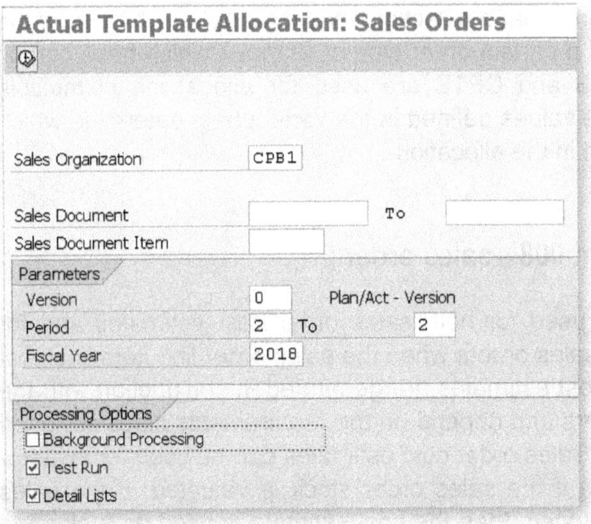

Figure 5.18: Sales order actual template allocation - CPTJ

5.2.9 Environment 009—process orders

Process orders are manufacturing orders for the process industry. Whereas production orders use BOMs and routes (task list type N) to define the manufacturing process, process orders use BOMs and recipes (task list type 2). The order category for process orders is 40. Environment 001 is used for both product costing and order costs for production orders (order category 10). Environment 009 only applies to costs directly associated with process orders. Standard cost estimates for materials manufactured using process orders continue to use environment 001 for template allocations. To ensure that the template allocation costs for the standard cost estimate match the allocations for the process orders, the template used for environment 009 must be in sync with the environment 001 template used for standard costing.

When a process order is created, the overhead key is transferred from the material to the order. The costing variants defined for the process orders are assigned to the order type just as they are for production orders and product cost collectors. The costing variants for the plan and simultaneous costing are shown on the CONTROL tab of the process order (transactions COR1/COR2/COR3). This is shown in Figure 5.19.

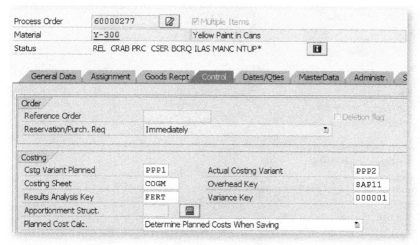

Figure 5.19: Control tab of the process order—COR1/COR2/COR3

The costing sheet is assigned to the valuation variant of each costing variant. The default costing variants are PPP1 for plan order costs and PPP2 for actual costs. The corresponding valuation variants are 006 and 007. The costing sheet and overhead key can be overridden when creating the order. Make sure that if a separate costing sheet is used for actual costs, both costing sheets are connected to the template via the overhead key. See Section 3.5 for details regarding the connection for production orders in environment 001. The connection of the template to the overhead key and costing sheet is configured using transaction KTPF.

The plan template allocation is generated when saving the process order. Actual costs must be allocated by running either transaction CPTA for a single order or CPTD for all orders at a plant. When running CPTD, make sure that the WITH PROCESS ORDERS checkbox is selected (see Figure 5.20). These are the same transactions used for environment 001 production orders.

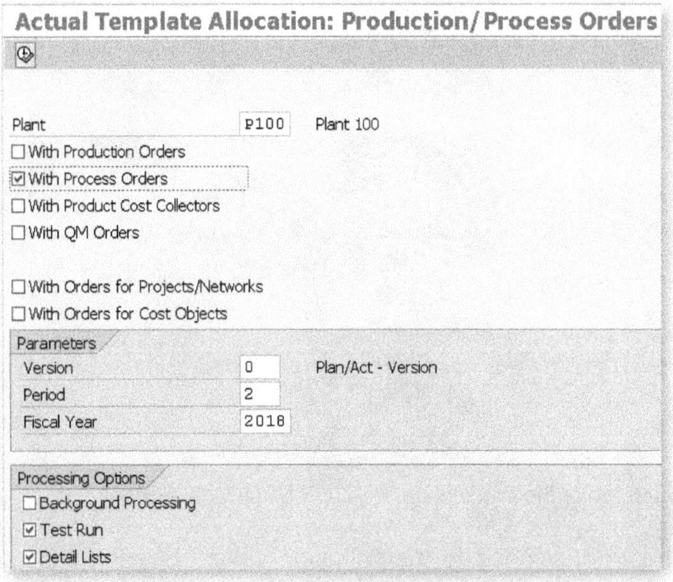

Figure 5.20: Multiple order template allocation for process orders

5.2.10 Environment 010—product cost collectors

Product cost collectors serve two different purposes. First, they are used to capture costs for repetitive manufacturing. Repetitive manufacturing describes production which does not use individual orders to distinguish quantities of planned output. Instead, production output is planned at a more macro level based on expected output on a time basis, such as a week or a month. In essence, repetitive manufacturing orders are standing orders that never end. Order costs are associated with the material assigned to the cost collector. The product cost collector serves as the repository of these order costs.

A second use for product cost collectors is to aggregate costs from individual production orders for a given material. In this case, the individual production order is no longer a cost object and the costs "pass through" the production order and are posted to the assigned product cost collector. This behavior is defined when configuring the production order type.

A product cost collector is assigned an order type in a similar manner to production orders and process orders. The order category for cost collectors is 5. A special costing variant is used to create the planned costs. The delivered costing variant for this is PREM, and it is attached to valuation variant 001. The default costing sheet is the one assigned to valuation variant 001, and the overhead key is transferred from the material. This is on the DATA tab of transaction KKF6N (see Figure 5.21).

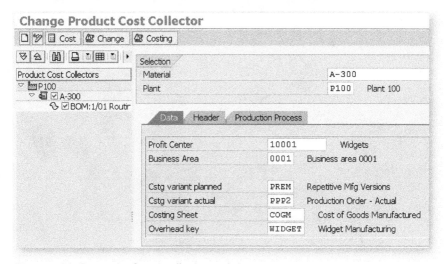

Figure 5.21: Data tab of cost collector maintenance

The costing sheet can be overridden when creating the cost collector, but normally the default costing sheet derived from the plan costing variant should be used. The costing variant used for actual costs is typically the same for both production orders and process orders, and the delivered valuation variant used for this is 007. This may have a different costing sheet assigned, and for the allocations to work properly, the environment 010 template and overhead key should be assigned to both costing sheets in configuration.

Preliminary cost estimates for the cost collector can be made using KKF6N or MF30. After creating a new cost collector, the system asks whether a cost estimate should be created. When making changes to a cost collector in KKF6N, use the ☐ Cost button to recreate the cost estimate before saving. Alternatively, MF30 can be used to create cost estimates for multiple cost collectors. This is especially useful if cost collectors were created using the mass create transaction KKF6M. Assuming the connection configuration was made using transaction KTPF, the template allocation is included in the preliminary cost estimate.

Actual template allocations are performed at period end using one of two transactions. Transaction CPTE is used to allocate to a single cost collector or material (see Figure 5.22).

Figure 5.22: Template allocation for a single cost collector

CPTD is the standard allocation transaction for all orders involving production at a plant level. Make sure WITH PRODUCT COST COLLECTORS is selected, as shown in Figure 5.23.

Actual Template Allocation: Production/Process Orders

Plant   P100   Plant 100
☐ With Production Orders
☐ With Process Orders
☑ With Product Cost Collectors
☐ With QM Orders

Figure 5.23: Production order template allocation - CPTD

5.2.11 Environment 011—service orders

Service orders, plant maintenance orders, and QM orders use environment 011. Order category 30 is used for service and plant maintenance orders, and category 6 is used for QM orders. Like production orders and process orders, maintenance orders are assigned two costing variants. One is for plan cost and the other is for actual costs. Special valuation variants configured for plant maintenance needs are assigned to the costing variants for plan and actual costing. When creating a maintenance order, the costing sheet is assigned from the valuation variant associated with the plan cost costing variant. The overhead key is manually assigned on the CONTROL tab of the order, as shown in Figure 5.24.

Figure 5.24: Maintenance order cost assignment

Plan costs are created when the order is saved using the costing variant assigned to CSTGVARIANTPLAN. Actual costs are allocated using transactions CPTA for single orders and CPTB for multiple orders. Figure 5.25 shows the selection of a single order using CPTA. A special selection variant needs to be set up to use CPTB for maintenance orders.

Figure 5.25: Single order template allocation—CPTA

QM orders are created with transaction QK04, and the costing sheet and overhead key are assigned when creating the order (see Figure 5.26).

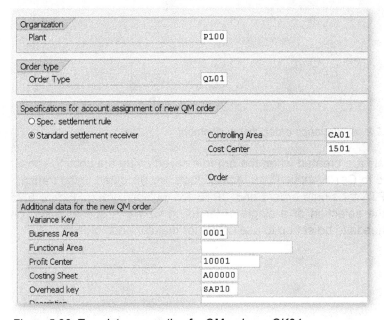

Figure 5.26: Template connection for QM orders—QK04

Transaction KKF2 is used for modifying QM orders, and when using this transaction, the costing definition is on the PRD-END CLOSING tab. See Section 5.2.12 for more details. Actual allocation for a single QM order uses transaction CPTA. However, these order types use transaction CPTD when allocating to multiple orders in a plant. Make sure that WITH QM ORDERS is selected when running that transaction (see Figure 5.27).

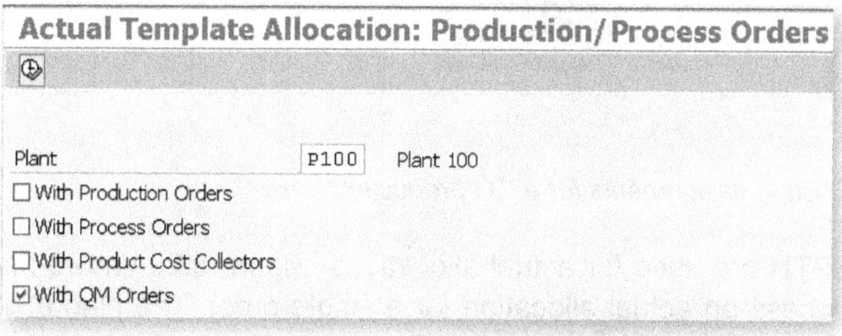

Actual Template Allocation: Production/Process Orders

Plant   P100   Plant 100
- ☐ With Production Orders
- ☐ With Process Orders
- ☐ With Product Cost Collectors
- ☑ With QM Orders

Figure 5.27: Multiple QM order template allocation—CPTD

5.2.12 Environment 012—CO production orders

CO production orders are production orders without quantity structure. No BOM or routing is used in processing these orders. The order category for CO production orders is 4.

The costing sheet is assigned in the PERIOD-END CLOSING section of the PRD-END CLOSING tab of the order maintenance transaction (KKF1/KKF2/KKF3). Figure 5.28 shows how this is defined. The default assignment comes from the valuation variant that is assigned to the costing variant defined for the order type. The overhead key is defined in the material master on the COSTING 1 tab. The costing sheet and overhead key can be overridden in the order. The connection to the template is configured using transaction KTPF.

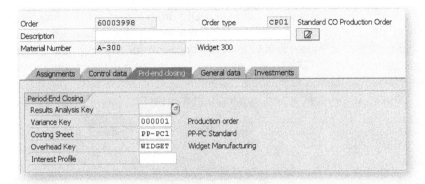

Figure 5.28: Costing assignments for a CO production order

CPTA and CPTD are used for actual allocations. Figure 5.29 shows the options to process an actual allocation for a single order. The plan allocations are generated when the cost estimate is saved with the order. When using CPTD, make sure that WITH PRODUCTION ORDERS is selected. CO production orders are processed like regular production orders.

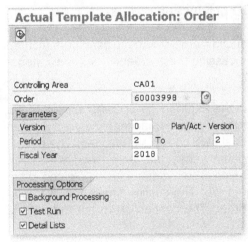

Figure 5.29: Single CO order template allocation - CPTA

5.3   ECP—Easy Cost Planning

Easy Cost Planning is used for generating cost estimates based on information assigned to characteristics defined in a costing model. The resulting cost estimate can be used to generate cost plans for projects, internal orders, and appropriations requests. There are special template environments for each of these. Ad hoc cost estimates can also be created using Easy Cost Planning. These can be used to give insight into costs for new products or services.

To aid in creating one of these cost estimates, a cost model must be set up first. The cost model is a combination of characteristics and a set of derivation rules (i.e. a template) that uses values assigned to the characteristics to generate costs in a cost estimate. Part of creating the model is assigning the characteristics to a data entry screen to load the data for the resulting cost calculations. Chapter 6 covers the details of creating the models and generating the cost estimates.

The templates used to define the derivation rules include many more row types than other templates, which allow for the assignment of costs from various sources to the final cost estimate. Costing sources include materials, internal and external activities, subcontracting, external services, directly assigned costs, and even other cost models. When used for ad hoc costing (environment 200), the result is a cost estimate that can represent a "what if" cost. Other types of Easy Cost Planning cost estimates can be transferred directly to a receiver cost object, such as a WBS element or internal order. Different environments are used for these types of cost estimates.

Easy Cost Planning environment templates cannot be created using the standard template maintenance transactions CPT1 and CPT2. Instead, there is a special costing model transaction CKCM that is used for model maintenance. Template maintenance in this transaction is only one part of what it can do. It is also used to create and assign characteristics for use in the model, as well as helping to structure how these characteristics are entered for use in the cost estimate. See Chapter 6 for a more detailed explanation of how cost models are set up and how the templates are used to generate the cost estimates.

5.4   CPI—formula planning

Formula planning is a means of creating cost plans for cost centers, business processes, and profit centers based on actual and plan data available in the system. Templates can have complex formulas that are used in the generation of the plan data. The CPI application covers formula planning for cost centers and business processes. Formula planning for Profit Center Accounting is a different template application and is covered in Section 5.7.

Unlike most other template applications, the output generated by processing formula planning templates is made up of the plan amounts for cost elements in the receiving cost objects. These receiving cost objects are either cost centers or business processes. Only plan costs are processed. Like standard cost center planning, formula planning can be activity-dependent or activity-independent. Activity-independent planning uses environment CPI templates and only requires that a cost center be assigned as the receiver object. These plan costs are fixed. Activity-dependent planning for cost centers (environment CPD) also requires specifying an activity type as the receiver object. Both fixed and variable costs can be planned in this manner. When using CPD environment templates, the plan allocation applies to all activity types planned for the receiver cost center unless a restriction is made in the ACTIVATION column. Business process planning (environment BPP) is considered activity-dependent, so fixed and variable costs can be used in planning for these objects as well. Figure 5.30 shows an example of a template for environment CPD.

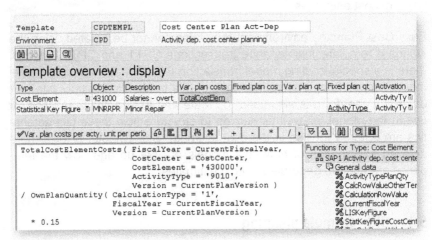

Figure 5.30: Formula planning template—environment CPD

The assignment of a template to the cost center is made in the cost center master data using the TEMPLATES tab in the FORMULA PLANNING section (see Figure 5.31). There is one option for an activity-independent template (❶) and another for activity-independent planning (❷).

Figure 5.31: Formula planning cost center assignment

Template allocation for business process formula planning uses environment BPP. There is only one type of formula planning template allowed, and this is assigned in the TEMPLATES tab in the FORMULA PLANNING section (see Figure 5.32).

Figure 5.32: Formula planning business process assignment

If the system is set up to enable the maintenance of templates in production, this can be done using the ▢ and ✎ buttons. The ✑ button can be used to view the template once it has been created.

Formula planning processing is performed by one of two transactions. KPT6 is used for both activity-dependent and activity-independent planning for cost centers. This is shown in Figure 5.33. CPT6 is the transaction for business process planning.

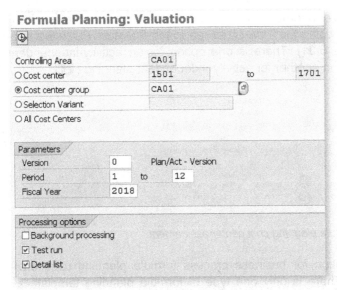

Formula Planning: Valuation

Controling Area	CA01		
○ Cost center	1501	to	1701
⦿ Cost center group	CA01		
○ Selection Variant			
○ All Cost Centers			

Parameters

Version	0	Plan/Act - Version	
Period	1	to	12
Fiscal Year	2018		

Processing options
- ☐ Background processing
- ☑ Test run
- ☑ Detail list

Figure 5.33: Transaction KPT6—formula planning

As a result of executing one of these transactions, a plan is loaded for the costing version specified in the template (see Figure 5.34).

Formula Planning: Results

Cost Ctr	ActTyp	Cost Element	Resource	StatKF	Fixed val.	Vbl. value	Quantity	Vbl. qty	E
1501	9010	431000			0.00	112,500.00	0.000	0.000	
1501	9010			MNRRPR	0.00	0.00	50.000	0.000	

Figure 5.34: KPT6 formula planning results

5.5 SBP—activity assignments

The SBP application includes several environments: the SBP environment for allocation to business processes, SCI for activity-independent cost centers, and SCD for activity-dependent cost centers. Both plan and actual allocations can be made using business processes and cost center/activity types as the senders. Planning using SBP application envi-

ronment templates is different to the formula planning of the CPI application because the allocation objects are activities or business processes
rather than cost elements.

Templates for SCD (activity-dependent) and SBP (business process)
environments allow for both variable and fixed allocation quantities. SCI
(activity-independent) only allows fixed allocation quantities because the
receiver is just a cost center. Figure 5.35 shows a template for environment SCD.

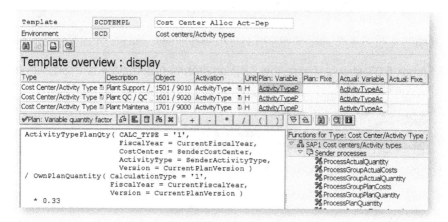

Figure 5.35: Activity allocation template—environment SCD

Unlike templates associated with the COB application, there is only one
activation method that is used for both plan and actual allocations.
Should a different set of criteria for a plan versus an actual allocation be
required, then two rows need to be created; one to handle only the plan
allocations and the other to handle only the actual allocations.

The templates are connected to the receiver cost centers or business
processes in the ACTIVITY AND BUSINESS PROCESS ALLOCATION section of
the TEMPLATES tab in the master data maintenance transaction (KS01 or
KS02 for cost centers, and CP01 or CP02 for business processes). Figure 5.36 shows the cost center definition using transaction KS02. There
is one selection for an activity-independent template (❶) and another
one for activity-independent planning (❷).

Figure 5.36: Activity allocation cost center assignment

Figure 5.37 shows where the SBP environment template is assigned in transaction CP02.

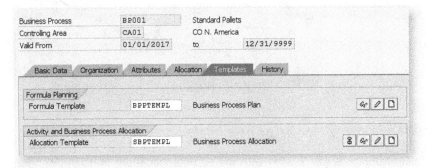

Figure 5.37: Activity allocation business process assignment

If the system is set up to enable the maintenance of templates in production, this can be done using the ☐ and ✎ buttons. The ✍ button can be used to view the template once it has been created.

The ░ button is used to display the allocation structure for the template. Figure 5.38 shows an example of an allocation structure for the SCD environment template.

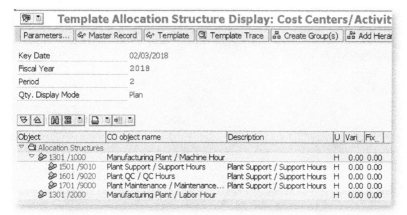

Figure 5.38: Allocation structure for the cost center

The Parameters... button is used to switch between actual and plan alloca-tion structures. The ℚ Template Trace button is used to display how the template is used in the allocation. This provides the same output as the template tracing functionality in the template maintenance transactions (covered in Section 3.6).

There are four allocation transactions which can be used, depending on which allocation is to be performed. KPAS is used for actual allocations for both activity-dependent and activity-independent templates. Transac-tion KPPS is used for the plan allocation to the cost center for environ-ments SCD and SCI. The corresponding transactions for business pro-cesses are CPAS (actual allocation) and CPPS (plan allocation).

Figure 5.39 shows how transaction KPPS is invoked. A set of cost cen-ters must be selected along with the period(s) and fiscal year for the postings. Checking TEST RUN runs the allocation without posting. DETAIL LISTS gives a report showing what was allocated.

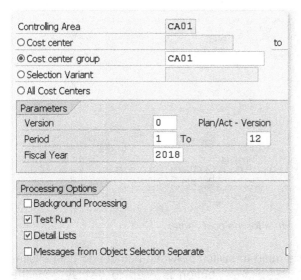

Figure 5.39: Transaction KPPS—plan activity allocation

Figure 5.40 shows the result of the allocation. Look at the receiver object to determine whether activity-dependent (object type ATY) or activity-independent (object type CTR) was used for cost center allocations.

Plan Template Allocation: Cost Centers/Activity Ty (Test Run)

Result

Receiver Object	Sender object	AllocCElem	Ttl v. qty	TotFxdQty	TotF&Vqty	UoM	Ttl F+V val.CAC	COCr	Template
ATY 1301/1000	ATY 1501/9010	943160	3,960.00	0.00	3,960.00	H	297,000.00	USD	SCDTEMPL
	ATY 1601/9020	943170	360.00	0.00	360.00	H	16,200.00	USD	SCDTEMPL
	ATY 1701/9000	943150	16.50	0.00	16.50	H	8,250.00	USD	SCDTEMPL
ATY 1301/1000							321,450.00	USD	
CTR 1301	ATY 1701/9000	943150	0.00	180.00	180.00	H	90,000.00	USD	SCITEMPL
CTR 1301							90,000.00	USD	
							411,450.00	USD	

Figure 5.40: KPPS activity allocation results

Section 1.3.4 also shows an example of a template actual allocation using transaction KPAS involving environment SCI.

5.6 SKI—statistical key figures

The SKI application is similar to SBP, but strictly deals with the posting of statistical key figures to cost centers. Only actual allocations are supported. The SKI environment is for allocations independent of activity. This means that the posting of the statistical key figure is made with reference only to the cost center. The SKD environment is dependent on the activity types planned for the cost center, and postings are made associated with all activity types assigned to the cost center. If two activity types are planned, then statistical key figure postings are made for both activity types unless constrained by the logic within the template. SKI environment allocations work in a similar manner to SCI environment allocations, and SKD allocations work in a similar manner to SCD allocations. The allocations for these environments result in statistical key figure postings to the receiver cost centers. Figure 5.41 shows an example of a template in the SKD environment.

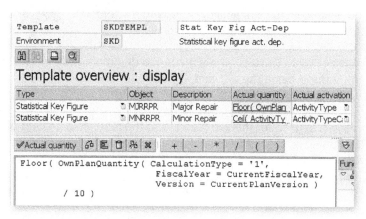

Figure 5.41: Statistical key figure template –SKD environment

Only actual statistical key figure quantities can be allocated using these two environments. Figure 5.42 shows the TEMPLATES tab for cost center maintenance using transaction KS02. These templates are assigned in the ACTUAL STATISTICAL KEY FIGURES section of the window.

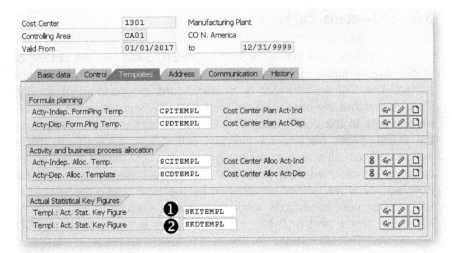

Figure 5.42: Statistical key figure cost center assignment

There is one selection for an activity-independent template (❶) and another one for activity-independent planning (❷).

If the system is set up to enable the maintenance of templates in production, this can be done using the ◻ and ⧸ buttons. The ✍ button can be used to view the template once it has been created.

Transaction KSSK is used for the allocation, and the result is a posting of statistical key figures at the cost center level. Figure 5.43 shows the selection window for transaction KSSK. A set of cost centers must be entered along with the period(s) and fiscal year for the postings. Choosing TEST RUN runs the allocation without posting. DETAIL LISTS gives a report showing what was allocated.

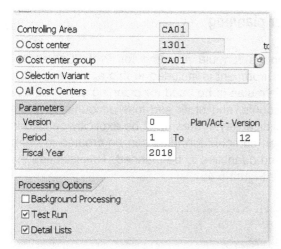

Figure 5.43: Transaction KSSK—statistical key figure allocation

The result of the allocation is shown in Figure 5.44.

Actual Template Allocation: Stat. Key Figure for C (Test Run)

Result

Receiver Object	StatKF	Alloc. CElem	Ttl v. qty	TotFxdQty	TotF&Vqty	UoM	Template
ATY 1301/1000	MNRRPR		11,964	0	11,964	EA	SKDTEMPL
ATY 1301/1000 ⟁							
ATY 1301/2000	MJRRPR		2,400	0	2,400	EA	SKDTEMPL
	MNRRPR		23,964	0	23,964	EA	SKDTEMPL
ATY 1301/2000 ⟁							
CTR 1301	MJRRPR		120	0	120	EA	SKITEMPL
CTR 1301 ⟁							
⟁							

Figure 5.44: KSSK statistical key figure allocation results

157

5.7 PCA—profit center planning

The PCA application supports formula planning for Profit Center Accounting. Only the PCA environment is included in this application. This enables the definitions of formulas to be used for planning statistical key figures, balance sheet accounts, and profit and loss accounts for profit centers. Accounts and statistical key figures must be explicitly defined in the template rows. However, complex formulas can be created in order to calculate the amounts and quantities to be planned. This includes the use of calculation rows (see Figure 5.45).

Template	PCPLAN	Profit Center Formula Plan				
Environment	PCA	Profit center planning				

Template overview : display

Type	Object	Description	Plan amount p	Planned quantit	Unit	Activation cond
Comment Row		Formula plan r				
Statistical Key Figure	MJRRPR	Major Repair		ActivityTypePla		ProfitCenterPe
P&L Account	476000	Office supplies	Cell(500			ProfitCenterPe
Balance Sheet Account	300000	Inventory - Ra	Abs (51234 *			CompanyCode

Figure 5.45: Profit center formula planning template

The template is assigned to the profit center in the INDICATORS tab (see Figure 5.46).

Figure 5.46: Profit center Indicators tab

Only environment PCA templates are allowed. If the system is configured to enable maintenance of templates in production, this can be done using the ☐ and ✐ buttons. The ✧ button can be used to view the template once it has been created.

Planning is executed using transaction 7KET (see Figure 5.47). Select the profit center(s) or profit center group for which the planning should be executed. Next, choose the planning version and time frame.

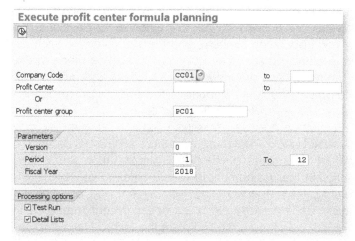

Figure 5.47: Transaction 7KET—formula planning

This can be executed in test mode first by selecting TEST RUN to see the results prior to posting. Select the DETAIL LISTS option to view the results.

Processing category	Number
Number of profit centers	1
Number of values determined	3

Figure 5.48: Summary report from 7KET

Drill into the summary report row that shows the number of values determined to see the postings (see Figure 5.48). The detail report shows the allocations (see Figure 5.49).

Formula Planning: Results

COAr	CoCd	Profit Ctr	StatKF	Account	Amount	Quantity	Crcy	BUn
CA01	CC01	10001		300000	182,034.40		USD	
CA01	CC01	10001		476000	6,060.00		USD	
CA01	CC01	10001	MJRRPR		0.00	1,000	USD	EA

Figure 5.49: Detail report from 7KET

5.8 PAC—costing based profitability analysis

The structures of costing-based CO-PA (Profitability Analysis) are dependent on an individual implementation, and rely on the characteristics and value fields that are defined for that implementation. Special tables are created for each operating concern, and the structures for each operating concern are unique. These structures must also be made available for use in templates and required special configuration procedures. Configuration for these structures is found in two places: CONTROLLING • PROFITABILITY ANALYSIS • PLANNING • INTEGRATED PLANNING • TRANSFER COST CENTER PLANNING/PROCESS PLANNING • SET UP TEMPLATE ALLOCATION, and in CONTROLLING • PROFITABILITY ANALYSIS • FLOWS OF ACTUAL VALUES • TRANSFER OF OVERHEAD • SET UP TEMPLATE ALLOCATION. Configuration begins with the assignment of record types to be used in the allocations. Select DEFINE RECORD TYPES FOR SELECTING COST DRIVERS from under the SET UP TEMPLATE ALLOCATION option in configuration. This is transaction KEVG (see Figure 5.50). Select the record types from the list provided.

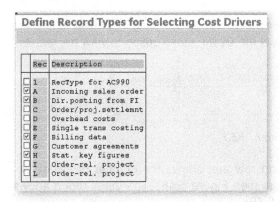

Rec	Description
1	RecType for AC990
A	Incoming sales order
B	Dir.posting from FI
C	Order/proj.settlemnt
D	Overhead costs
E	Single trans costing
F	Billing data
G	Customer agreements
H	Stat. key figures
I	Order-rel. project
L	Order-rel. project

Figure 5.50: Defining record types for allocations—KEVG

Next, select the characteristics that are to be used in the update. This is handled in the SPECIFY CHARACTERISTICS FOR SELECTION AND UPDATE option under SET UP TEMPLATE ALLOCATION (transaction KEAS). Figure 5.51 shows the three characteristics that are used for template allocations for operating concern IDEA. These characteristics are added to the CO-PA template allocation transactions as selection options.

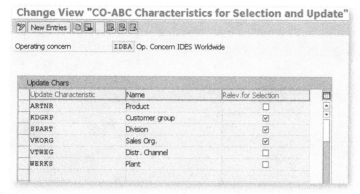

Figure 5.51: Defining characteristics for allocations—KEAS

After completing the above configuration, generate the structures to be used for the updates. This is done with the GENERATE TEMPLATE ENVIRONMENT FOR CO-PA option under SET UP TEMPLATE ALLOCATION (transaction KEAE).

Template connection is made by defining the list of rules used for template allocations in transaction KEKW (option MAINTAIN TEMPLATE DETERMINATION AND OTHER UPDATE CHARACTERISTICS under SET UP TEMPLATE ALLOCATION). When defining the rules, click on the ⊞ Maintain Rule Values button to get to the template assignment, as shown in Figure 5.52. Different templates can be assigned to different characteristics.

Template determination and other update characteristics: Change Rule V

Determination R

No value filter active

Cus	Customer group Name	Divi	Division Name	Sales	Sales Organization Name	Assi	Template	Template Name
01	Industrial customers	00	Cross-division	CPB1	Sales Org. US	⬛	PACTEMPL	CO-PA Template
06	Competition	10	Vehicles	CPF1	Sales Org. US	⬛	CBF1SALES	Template for Sale Org CBF1

Figure 5.52: Template connections—KEKW

Environment PAC supports both plan and actual template allocations. CPPE is used for transferring plan data and CPAE is used for actual data. The look of these transactions is affected by the configuration of the characteristics to be used for template allocation. Figure 5.53 shows that Customer group, Division, and Sales Org have been configured in transaction KEAS as characteristics that can be selected to define which allocations are to be processed.

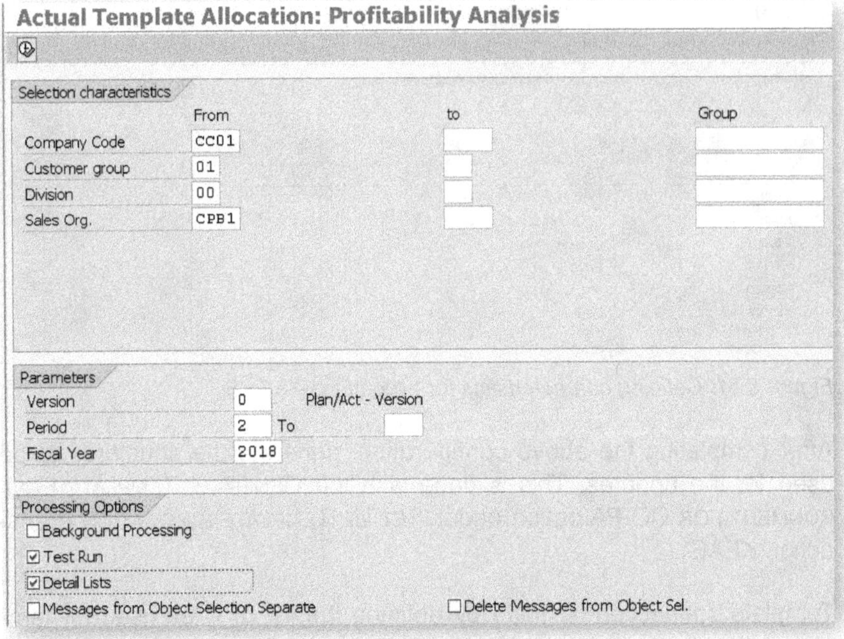

Actual Template Allocation: Profitability Analysis

Selection characteristics

	From	to	Group
Company Code	CC01		
Customer group	01		
Division	00		
Sales Org.	CPB1		

Parameters

Version	0	Plan/Act - Version
Period	2	To
Fiscal Year	2018	

Processing Options
- ☐ Background Processing
- ☑ Test Run
- ☑ Detail Lists
- ☐ Messages from Object Selection Separate   ☐ Delete Messages from Object Sel.

Figure 5.53: Actual allocations using CPAE

5.9 SOP—transfer sales and operation plan

Sales and Operation Planning (SOP) is a tool which creates sales, production, and other supply chain targets that are generated using historical data and forecasts. Activity plans for cost centers can be transferred from the resulting plan version. A template can be used in the calculation of the activity plan based on the sales and operation plan. The template is created in environment SOP. Figure 5.54 shows an example of an SOP template.

The object for these types of templates refers to the receiver of the plan allocation quantity.

The plan is based on the quantity of each material that is included in the SOP plan. The template connection is made through the overhead key assigned to the materials in the plan. The assignment of the overhead key is made using transaction KTPF, similar to the connection for costing (see Figure 5.55).

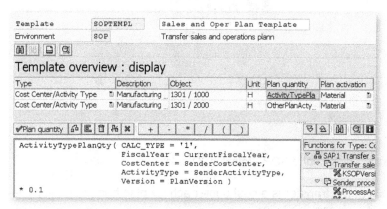

Figure 5.54: Template for transferring SOP plan

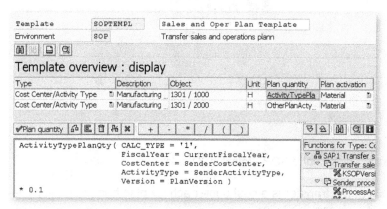

Figure 5.55: SOP template assignment to overhead key

When configuring the connection between the overhead key and the SOP environment template, no costing sheet should be defined. Any assignment using a costing sheet is assumed to be associated with COB application templates.

Transaction KSOP is used to transfer the plan. Enter the plant, the SOP version, and the fiscal planning information (see Figure 5.56).

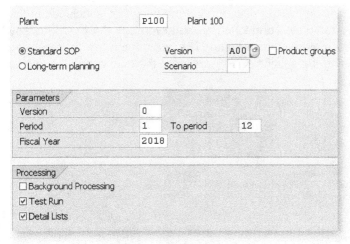

Figure 5.56: Transaction KSOP—transfer SOP plan

The result of the transfer is a cost center activity plan based on the material quantities in the SOP plan.

5.10 ISB—financial objects

The SAP Strategic Enterprise Management Banking module (SEM Banking) contains an interface to CO-PA. This is used for the calculation of revenue of individual transactions, and it provides a reporting system for looking at profitability by market segment or business area. Values can be transferred from the CO module using assessments and template allocations of business process costs. The special ISB application contains several environments associated with various types of banking accounts. A list of these environments can be found in Table 7.2 in the appendix.

The templates are used to allocate quantities of business processes into Profitability Analysis value fields based on activity for the various account types. Figure 5.57 shows an example of a template from the BSV (services) environment.

Figure 5.57: Template in the BSV (banking services) environment

The connection of a costing rule to a specific template is a part of the SEM Banking configuration, using transaction JBT1. Each costing rule is assigned a transaction type and other parameters which are used to identify the template environment for the allocations. A list of templates can be assigned on the TEMPLATE tab of transaction JBT1, as shown in Figure 5.58.

Figure 5.58: Template connection in rule maintenance—JBT1

This is used as an interface to CO-PA. The characteristics and value fields associated with the allocations must be configured using transaction JBPD (see Figure 5.59).

Operating concern	IDEA	Op. Concern IDES Worldwide

Update Characteristics IS-B: CO-OM-ABC -> CO-PA	
Characteristic	Description
WWSBU	Strategic Bus.Unit

Figure 5.59: Characteristic configuration for SEM banking

165

Transaction JBKW is used during period end for processing the allocations associated with the costing rules. Select one or more types of financial object from the list provided at the top of the selection window.
Then, select the business processes and the fiscal time frame involved
with the allocation (see Figure 5.60). The resulting allocation updates the
specific value fields in CO-PA.

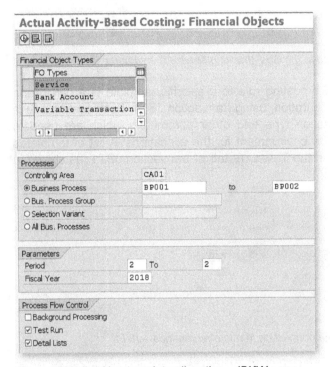

Figure 5.60: Banking template allocation - JBKW

A review of the S/4HANA simplification lists indicates that this functionality is no longer available. SEM banking, of which this is a part, is being
disabled. Refer to SAP notes 2211665[5], 2270318[6], and 2270530[7] for
further information about this. Transactions still appear to be available,
but the menu paths have been deleted.

---

[5] Note 2211665 - Release information for "SAP for Banking" in connection with "SAP
S/4HANA, on-premise edition 1511"

[6] Note 2270318—S4TWL—SEM Banking

[7] Note 2260530—S4TWL—Several Kinds of Financial Objects Disabled

6 Easy Cost Planning

Easy Cost Planning was briefly introduced in Chapter 5. It uses template structures for defining derivation rules used for calculating costs. Instead of calculating quantities for allocation as is the norm with other template applications, Easy Cost Planning uses the template structure to determine costs based on various characteristics that are assigned to a cost model. The result of combining the values entered for the model characteristics with the derivation rules is a cost estimate itemization which can be used as an ad hoc cost or for planning costs for WBS elements or internal orders. This chapter looks at how templates are used to create the cost estimates.

6.1 Easy Cost Planning scenario

Easy Cost Planning is a very flexible tool used to create cost estimates that are used for planning costs for certain CO objects, and also for generating ad hoc costs used in "what if" analyses. A full examination of Easy Cost Planning and its uses is beyond the scope of this book. This chapter concentrates on creating costing models and how the templates are used as part of these costing models.

To highlight how Easy Cost Planning templates are defined and used, an ad hoc costing scenario for forecasting manufacturing costs for the widgets presented in Chapter 2 is used. Management wants to determine how changes in BOM and manufacturing parameters will affect the cost of manufacturing. Key manufacturing processes and simulation requirements are listed below:

▶ Widgets are made with up to 4 different components, and there may be multiple amounts of each component included in the BOM. Management wants to be able to look at both existing raw materials in stock as well as new raw materials in order to determine the material cost of the widget.

- ▶ It takes 3 minutes to manufacture a widget using the current process. Management wants to know the cost impact of changing the manufacturing speed and also account for different equipment for manufacturing the widget.

- ▶ Setting up the current machine takes 2 hours. Management wants to know the cost impact if this time is changed.

- ▶ Recalibration time takes 30 minutes and must be done for every 100 widgets that are manufactured. Management wants to determine the impact of changing the recalibration time on the cost of manufacturing.

- ▶ Quality inspection takes 30 seconds for non-dangerous goods components and twice as long for dangerous goods components. Management wants to know how changing the inspection time will impact on the product cost.

- ▶ Pallets can currently hold 250 kg. Management wants to know the effect of changing the quantities that can be packed per pallet.

Based on these requirements, a costing model is built using characteristics to store the important parameters of the model, and derivation rules which are used to combine the values entered to create a cost estimate for the model. The derivation rules are actually an environment 200 template. The next sections cover how models are created and used to generate the ad hoc cost estimate.

6.2 Costing models

The cost estimates coming from Easy Cost Planning are structured based on a costing model defined with transaction CKCM. A costing model consists of a set of characteristics, a data entry screen to assign values to the characteristics, and derivation rules to determine how the characteristics are used to calculate the costs.

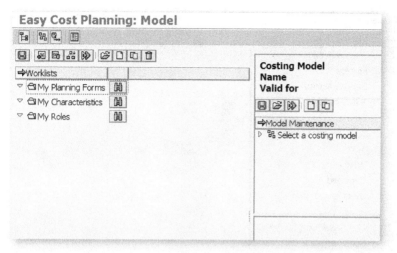

Figure 6.1: Initial screen for maintaining costing models CKCM

There are three windows in the costing model maintenance screen (see Figure 6.1). On the left side of the screen is the WORKLISTS window, which shows a set of models or planning forms, characteristics, and roles that are currently being worked on. The window on the upper right portion of the screen is for model selection, and once the model is selected, it displays the menu of the three modeling tasks (creating characteristics, structuring the screen, and defining the derivation rules). The lower right window shows either the list of characteristics or the model entry screen structure, depending on which function is selected. Derivation rule maintenance uses a separate template maintenance window.

The ⊞ button is used for toggling the display of the worklist window. If the window is displayed, clicking on this button hides the display and the two model maintenance windows are expanded. If the window is not being displayed, clicking this button causes the worklist window to be displayed. The ⊞ button displays the cost model windows. Click on this button to return to the cost model if the roles authorization window is currently active. The ⊞ switches from the model maintenance view to the roles authorization view. The ⊞ button is used to display the list of icons that are used for a cost model. Figure 6.2 shows the icons that are used in cost estimates as well as the item type for the resulting cost item in the itemization.

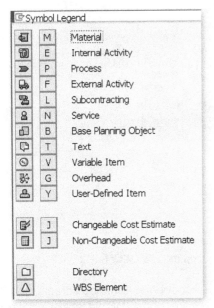

Figure 6.2: Icons used by the cost model

6.2.1 Worklists

The left window of Figure 6.1 is used for managing worklists. When developing cost models, worklists can be useful for easy access to those items that are currently under development. Worklists exist in three areas: models, characteristics, and role assignment. The worklists take up screen space, but this area can be hidden using the ⊞ button. Clicking on the same button again restores the worklist window.

Items can be added or removed from the worklist. To add an item, select the worklist area (MY PLANNING FORMS, MY CHARACTERISTICS, or MY ROLES). Click on the ⊞ button. Enter the item to be added or select it from a dropdown list. The list that is displayed is dependent on which worklist area is selected. This item is added to the end of the worklist. To remove an item from the worklist, first select it by clicking on the icon on the line. Then, click on the ⊞ button to remove the item from the list. The item itself is not deleted, but is just removed from the worklist. Each worklist area can also have sub-folders to better arrange the worklist. Sub-folders can be added by first selecting the worklist area and then clicking on the 🔧 button to insert the folder. There is a provision for re-naming a directory by using the ⏩ button.

Multiple worklists can be developed and saved independently of each other. The 📂 button opens an existing worklist item. The 🗋 button creates a new worklist. A worklist is copied to a new worklist by using the 🔲 button. This saves the selected worklist with a new name. When changes to a worklist are complete, click on the 💾 in the worklist window to save it. To delete a worklist, select the worklist ID and click on the 🗑 button.

6.2.2   Model maintenance window

New models can be created, or existing models can be viewed or changed. If the model maintenance windows are not displayed, click on the 🔳 button. To create a new model, click on the 🗋 button. To view or modify an existing model, click on the 📂 button in the model mainte-nance window to select and open the model. Alternatively, if the model is saved in the worklist, click on the model ID there to call up that model. When maintenance is complete, click on the 💾 button in the model maintenance window to save the model. To copy a model or save the changes under a new model name, click on the 🔲 button. The ⏩ but-ton is used to rename a model. The detailed description defining the characteristics, screen design, and derivation rules of a model is found in Sections 6.3 through 6.5.

6.2.3   Roles maintenance window

Certain functionality that is available in the Easy Cost Planning costing transaction CKECP can be disabled based on a security role. Switch to roles maintenance mode by clicking on the 🔖 button. This focus is changed from model maintenance to roles maintenance. The security role must be selected first. This could be either a single or composite role. The options are displayed in Figure 6.3.

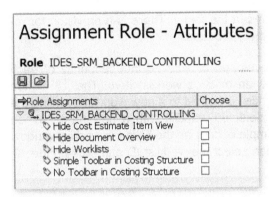

Figure 6.3: Role assignment options

The options are described in the following list:

▶ HIDE COST ESTIMATE ITEM VIEW—select this option to hide the itemization view in CKECP. The ✏ Show/Hide Item View button is then disabled. This means that the itemization cannot be viewed, and no manual changes can be made to the cost estimate.

▶ HIDE DOCUMENT OVERVIEW—select this option to disable access to the document flow for Execution Services. The ⬚ button is then hidden in the costing structure in CKECP.

▶ HIDE WORKLISTS—select this option to disable the use of work-lists in the cost estimate. The ⬚ button is then hidden in the costing structure in CKECP.

▶ SIMPLE TOOLBAR IN COSTING STRUCTURE—select this option to enable the simple toolbar for the costing structure. The simple toolbar excludes all itemization editing icons.

▶ NO TOOLBAR IN COSTING STRUCTURE—select this option to disable the toolbar in the costing structure in CKECP.

6.3 Assigning characteristics

The first step in creating a costing model is to assign the characteristics which are used for inputting the parameters that make up the cost. A *characteristic* in SAP is an extension of master data that allows for the specification of additional properties that can be assigned to an object. Characteristics are assigned to a class which represents the type of master data with which they are associated. Groups of characteristics are assigned to a specific class, and the class is used to associate its characteristics to a specific piece of master data. Classes are further assigned to a class type, which identifies the ultimate use of the characteristics. For example, class type 001 is for the material master, and the use of characteristics enables additional data to be defined for a material that is not accounted for in the standard material master tables. As an example, material color could be assigned to a characteristic, and the specific color assigned to a material can drive behavior for how that material is manufactured and handled. Characteristic classes cover a wide variety of master data, including batches, vendors, task lists, and variant configurations. A characteristic uses an internal name, which is required to access the value of that characteristic in the template. It also has a description which is displayed when assigning a value to that characteristic in Easy Cost Planning. For example, characteristic **ECP-COMPONENT-1** is the internal ID for the characteristic COMPONENT 1, which is what the person creating the cost estimate sees when entering values for the characteristics.

Using transaction CT04 is the normal way to maintain characteristics, and Easy Cost Planning characteristics can be maintained using that transaction. However, the costing model transaction CKCM interfaces to CT04 when creating or modifying characteristics, and this is the normal process to be used for maintaining characteristics for a costing model. Only under special circumstances is it necessary to create characteristics using CT04 (see Section 6.3.2). Make sure the characteristics window is displayed. If it is not, select ASSIGN CHARACTERISTICS TO THE MODEL, which is the first menu option under WIDGET in Figure 6.4.

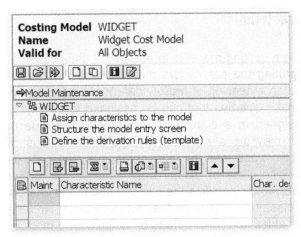

Figure 6.4: Initial windows for model maintenance

Any characteristics assigned to the model are displayed. Existing characteristics can be selected to be used by the model, existing characteristics can be modified, and new characteristics can be created.

6.3.1 Creating a characteristic in the model

Click on the ☐ button to create a characteristic. The window shifts to characteristic maintenance. Enter the name of the characteristic. The BASIC DATA tab is displayed. Assign a description to the characteristic. This description will be used in the model entry screen. The characteristic can also be assigned to a characteristic group, which is a useful way of categorizing it for use in searches. Select the group from the dropdown menu. Figure 6.5 shows that **ECP-COMPONENT-1** is assigned to the characteristics group "Widget Characteristics".

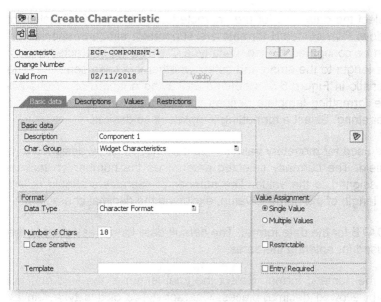

Figure 6.5: Basic data tab for characteristic maintenance

Searching for a characteristic

The same characteristic can be used in multiple costing models. There are several ways to find a characteristic to use in a model. Characteristics can be assigned to a characteristic group when maintaining the master data. Characteristic groups are configured in: CROSS-APPLICATION COMPONENTS • CLASSIFICATION SYSTEM • CHARACTERISTICS • DEFINE CHARACTERISTICS GROUPS. Assign like characteristics to the same group in order to more easily find specific characteristics. Another search method is to list the characteristics assigned to a class. The class assignment is made when the characteristic is defined for a model. The model name becomes the class.

Next, select the data type for the characteristic in the FORMAT section of the window. Five standard formats are supported, although special formats can be configured for use. Data type **CHAR** is for character strings. Assign a length to the string and select whether it is case-sensitive. The characteristic in Figure 6.5 is defined as having a length of 18 characters. The formatting template defines special rules for the format of the character string. Select a formatting template, if so desired.

CURR is used for monetary values. The currency must be assigned to a **CURR** field. The currency selected determines the number of decimal places assigned to the value. The number of characters should reflect the total length of the numeric value, excluding the decimal character.

Select **DATE** for the date format. The default date format assigned to the user is used for entering the dates.

NUM is the numeric format. Select the total length of the field and the number of allowed decimal places. Characteristics of this type can be used in formulas. A unit of measure can be assigned to this type of characteristic (see Figure 6.6).

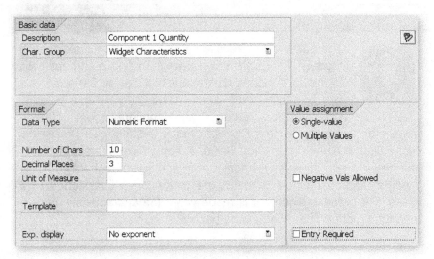

Figure 6.6: Options for numeric fields

The final data type is **TIME**. This is used for the entry of clock time.

The VALUE ASSIGNMENT section further defines how the characteristic can be used. A characteristic can be single-valued or multiple-valued. Single-valued characteristics are only assigned one value at a time. A multiple-valued characteristic can have more than one value assigned to it. Characteristics can be set as RESTRICTABLE, meaning that only certain allowed values can be assigned to the characteristic. If ENTRY REQUIRED is selected, then a value must be assigned to this characteristic.

The DESCRIPTIONS tab is used for entering characteristic descriptions in multiple languages (see Figure 6.7). Enter the language ID and the description in that particular language.

Figure 6.7: Descriptions tab in characteristic maintenance

Values entered for a characteristic can be checked for validity. This is done on the VALUES tab. Each allowable value and its description can be maintained in this area. When used in the data entry screen, these characteristics have a dropdown menu assigned, which provides a list of the values to select from.

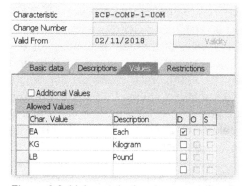

Figure 6.8: Values tab showing pre-defined values

The allowed entries in the VALUES tab depend on the data type of the characteristic. The **CHAR** data type does not allow ranges of values.

Only specific values can be defined. Figure 6.8 shows a listing of the valid unit of measure values for data entry in the cost estimation. Only these specific values are allowed for this characteristic.

The **TIME** data type displays values using the format HH:MM:SS. When defining valid values for this data type, the colons are removed, and values are represented as HHMMSS; for example, 12:01:01 would be represented as 120101, and 1:23:54 would be represented as 012354. The leading 0 is necessary for the hour portion. After entering the value, it is converted to the standard time format.

The **DATE** data type displays the date in the format defined in the user preferences. The validation values used for this data type depend on the date format selected. The separators must be removed, as this is entered as a number, but the value could represent MMDDYYYY or YYYYMMDD or some other combination of year, month, and day. A check is made to determine that the proper format has been used and after entering the value, it is converted to the standard date format.

Enter the value for the **CURR** data type. The currency defined for the characteristic is automatically assigned after entering the value.

Validation values can also be entered for the **NUM** data type, similar to the other data type. If a unit of measure is defined for the characteristic, the unit of measure is displayed as well.

For all the above data types, only one value can be entered per line. Ranges can be established for **DATE**, **TIME**, and **CURR** because numeric operators can be assigned to the value of the characteristic. For example, to allow all times after 12:00:00, make the entry **> 120000** and this allows all times greater than 12:00:00. Valid operators for single numbers are **>**, **>=**, **<**, and **<=**. To constrain values to a certain range, place a dash (-) after the first value and then enter a second value that is larger than the first. A range of between 12:00 and 16:00 is written as **120000—160000**. If 16:00 should not be included, then it is defined as **120000 - <160000**. To exclude the lower range value, the **>** operator can be used. To use intervals in the validation, the "multiple-value" setting should be defined on the BASIC DATA tab. Multiple intervals can be defined.

The RESTRICTIONS tab is used for assigning the characteristic to one or more class types. The class type definition determines in which applications the characteristic can be used. When creating the characteristic using transaction CKCM, class type 051 for Easy Cost Planning is automatically assigned. The characteristic in Figure 6.9 can only be used for Easy Cost Planning models.

Basic data	Descriptions	Values	Restrictions

Valid Class Types

Class Type	Description
051	Costing model

Figure 6.9: Characteristics class restrictions

6.3.2 Creating a characteristic using CT04

Characteristic maintenance in transaction CKCM does not include all options available when using the standard transaction CT04. Characteristics created directly in CKCM can be used in formulas and activation methods, but cannot be used for object determination. Having the ability to define an allocation object as a characteristic makes models more flexible to use. When creating a characteristic using CT04, the ADDNL DATA tab is made available (see Figure 6.10).

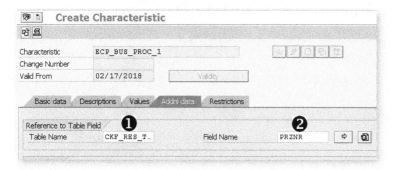

Figure 6.10: Additional data tab in transaction CT04

The characteristic can be assigned to a reference table (❶) and field (❷). To use a characteristic to define a value for activation, the table should be set to `CKF_RES_TPL` and the field should refer to the field in that structure that is associated with the object type for the activation. Table 7.17 in the appendix lists the fields in structure `CKF_RES_TPL`.

Object determination with structure CKF_RES_TPL

 Structure `CKF_RES_TPL` enables the use of model characteristics to define a specific object in the object determination column. When defining an object determination that uses the value of a model characteristic, two criteria must be fulfilled. First, there needs to be a Field Reference function that uses the same data type as a specific field in the structure. For certain objects that are specific to Easy Cost Planning, this must be assigned to a field in `CKF_RES_TPL`. Second, the characteristic that supplies the description of the object must have been created using transaction CT04. On the ADDNL DATA tab of characteristic maintenance, the characteristic is assigned to the specific `CKF_RES_TPL` field used by the object. This enables the characteristic "function" generated for the model to be used in object determination as well as activation. The resulting object determination method is shown in Figure 6.11 (`SenderProcess IN ECP_BUS_PROC_1`). The `SenderProcess` function is used for business process object determination, and `ECP_BUS_PROC_1` is the model characteristic created with CT04 that is assigned to field PRZNR, which uses the business process data type.

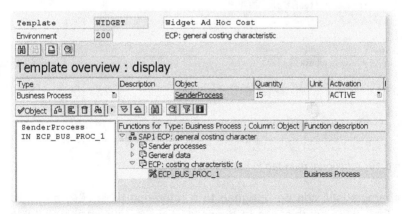

Figure 6.11: Use of characteristics in object determination

Class type for Easy Cost Planning characteristics

 The class type for Easy Cost Planning characteristics is 051. However, when creating or modifying a characteristic using transaction CT04, 051 does not show up as a valid class type. The class types are assigned on the RESTRICTIONS tab, and when using the dropdown selection or entering F4 in the class field to get the list of valid class types, 051 does not show up. It is still a valid class type and can be manually entered, if so desired. When using CKCM to create a characteristic, class type 051 is automatically assigned on the RESTRICTIONS tab of the characteristic definition.

6.3.3 Maintaining characteristics

New characteristics do not always need to be created for a new costing model. Existing characteristics can be reused from model to model. To use an existing characteristic, either type it in to the CHARACTERISTIC NAME cell, or use the dropdown menu to select the characteristic from the list.

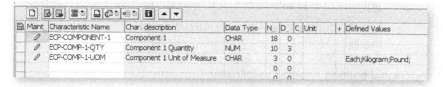

Figure 6.12: List of characteristics for the model

Using the same characteristic in multiple models

 Using the same characteristic in several models can have some drawbacks. If a model is created with sub-models, and the sub-models use some of the same characteristics as the top-level model, then when the value is entered at the top level, it will have the same value at all levels where it is referenced. This may or may not be an issue depending on how the model is being used.

Figure 6.12 shows the list of characteristics associated with the model. The order of the characteristics in the maintenance screen is important. This is the order that is used when the data is entered for the cost estimates. The characteristics can be modified, removed, or rearranged using the following editing buttons:

▶ The ⟋ button is used for modifying a specific characteristic. Click on this button to the left of the characteristic and the maintenance window is displayed. Make any changes necessary and save.

▶ The ⊟ button is used for removing a characteristic from the model. The characteristic is not deleted, but it is not used in the model. The characteristic must not be referenced in any cost estimate using that model.

▶ Clicking on the ⊞ button opens a line at the cursor position in the list of characteristics. First, select the line before which the characteristic is to be added. Type in the name of the characteristic to be added. This can be selected from the dropdown menu in the characteristic cell. If a new characteristic is to be added, click on the ⃞ button to create the new characteristic.

▶ The ▲ button moves the selected characteristic upward in the list. First select the characteristic's line, then click on this button until the characteristic is in the desired position.

▶ The ▼ button moves the selected characteristic downward in the list.

Additional buttons enable the following functions:

▶ Σ⊡ provides a special function for analyzing the lengths of the characteristics. Three calculation types are supported: mean value (the default), minimum value, and maximum value.

▶ ⊟ is used for printing the list of characteristics.

▶ ⌗⊡ is the Switch Views button. Only the grid style is supported.

▶ ⊞⊡ is used for changing the list layout.

▶ ⓘ displays documentation for the characteristic, if it has been created.

182

6.4   Structure the model entry screen

After the characteristics have been assigned to the model, the look of the data entry screen can be configured. Click on STRUCTURE THE MODEL ENTRY SCREEN (highlighted in Figure 6.13).

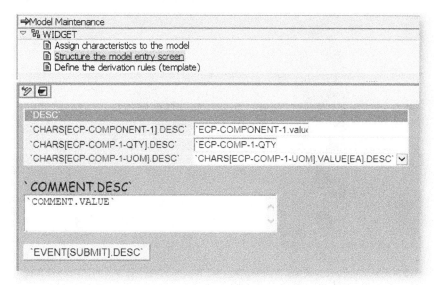

Figure 6.13: Initial window for structuring the entry screen

This window shows how the data entry looks when creating a cost esti- mate. 'DESC' in the title bar is replaced by the name given to the cost estimate. Below the title bar is the layout of the characteristic descrip- tions and values to be entered for those characteristics. 'CHARS[ECP- COMPONENT-1].DESC' is replaced with the description of characteristic **ECP-COMPONENT-1**. The description for this characteristic is "Compo- nent 1" (see Figure 6.5), and this is displayed on the data entry screen for the cost estimate.

The standard display can be changed by editing the HTML procedure associated with the data entry screen. Click on the 📎 button to bring up a window showing that HTML. An edit window is displayed for updating the HTML text. This is shown in Figure 6.14.

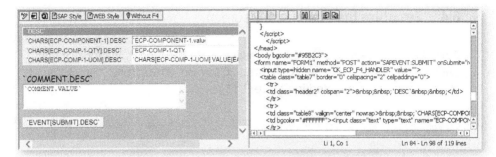

Figure 6.14: Model entry screen structure with HTML

Editing the HTML code requires some technical expertise, but changing descriptions is something that is not very difficult to do.

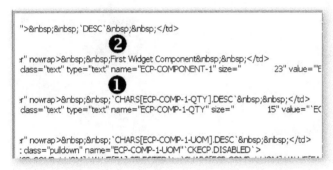

Figure 6.15: Modifying entry screen prompts in HTML

The HTML window is a simple editor through which changes can be made. Care must be taken when using it. Figure 6.15 shows how the default characteristic description can be changed. Section ❶ shows the second characteristic with its initial description `'CHARS[ECP-COMP-1-QTY].DESC'`. This indicates that the description associated with the definition of characteristic **ECP-COMP-1-QTY** will be used as the prompt on the model window. Section ❷ shows that the first parameter uses `First Widget Component` as the prompt. Note that in the first section, the text between the semicolons is enclosed with single-quotation marks. This indicates to the system that the description is to be derived from the description assigned to the characteristics in brackets. The second section does not have the description in quotation marks and the description in this case becomes the literal characters between the quotation marks. Be careful when making editing changes to the HTML code. Do not inadvertently delete the variables for the field values. If this is done, the val-

184

ues of the characteristics will not be available. These variables are generated in the form of '<CHARACTERISTIC_NAME>.value' or '<CHARACTERISTIC_NAME>.name'. The system replaces the variables with the value entered. The entire expression for the variable must not exceed one line.

The 🖳 button is used to transfer the edited HTML code to the model. Any changes that were made in the HTML editor are reflected in the data entry screen window. The result is shown in Figure 6.16.

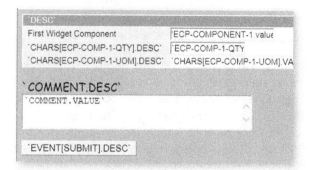

Figure 6.16: Updated model entry descriptions

The HTML code can be exported to a text file so that it can be modified by a more sophisticated HTML editor. This saved text file can also be used as a backup. Click on the 📄 button to save the HTML code to a local file. After the file has been modified, it can be uploaded back to the model using the 📄 button.

Reusing characteristics

Characteristics can be used in multiple models. The ability to change the default text when creating the model entry screen allows for a great deal of flexibility in reusing characteristics and reduces the necessity to continue creating new characteristics for each model.

The model entry screen can be refreshed using the original characteristic descriptions by selecting the 🖹SAP Style button. This restores the original descriptions that were shown in Figure 6.13. 🖹WEB Style is used to restructure the data entry screen using a web style. Any HTML code that has been manually changed is overwritten with the default characteristic definitions. Any custom changes need to be manually updated.

Restructuring the data entry screen

 If the characteristics have been changed for a model, it becomes necessary to restructure the data entry screen. Any manual changes to the HTML code are then lost. This includes any changes in the use of the [F4] button for those characteristics for which it is enabled. Special descriptions or other customizations need to be reloaded in the HTML code.

Unless enabled, there is no help for entering values for the characteristics defined in the model. Characteristics that have been assigned to certain fields in the CKF_RES_TPL structure can have this help enabled. If the ⚲Without F4 is displayed, click on it to enable an F4 button next to those characteristics. Click on ▤SAP Style or ▤WEB Style to regenerate the data entry screen. ⚲With F4 replaces the original button. Click on that button and regenerate the data entry screen to remove the F4 button. When the F4 button is enabled, click on that button to bring up the standard search window for the data type assigned to the characteristic. For example, if a characteristic is assigned to table CKF_RES_TPL, field PRZNR (business process), then the F4 button is displayed on the data entry screen next to the characteristic, and clicking on that button brings up the search window for cost centers (see Figure 6.17).

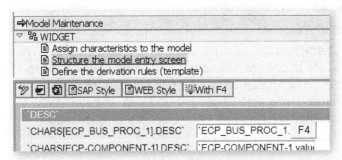

Figure 6.17: Enabling the F4 button for a characteristic

The resulting data entry screen in transaction CKECP also shows the button (see Figure 6.18). Clicking on the F4 button brings up the standard SAP search screen for the object type.

Figure 6.18: Cost estimate showing F4 button

When the automatically generated HTML code is changed, it is saved as a file using Business Document Services. The button brings up the Business Document Navigator, and this provides access to the saved files. Figure 6.19 shows the changed HTML template stored in the Business Document Navigator.

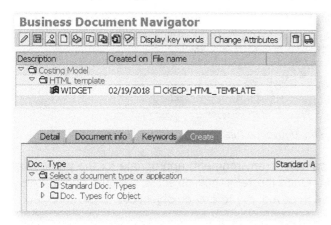

Figure 6.19: Business document manager

6.5 Define derivation rule templates

Easy Cost Planning uses derivation rules in conjunction with model characteristics to create a cost estimate. The derivation rules are the rows of a template. Four different environments are supported when creating a model. Select one of the following objects from the REFER-ENCE OBJECT dropdown menu shown in Figure 6.20:

▶ ALL OBJECTS—used for ad hoc cost estimates (environment 200)

▶ APPROPRIATION REQUEST—used for appropriation requests (environment 215)

▶ INTERNAL ORDERS—used for internal order cost planning (environment 207)

▶ WBS ELEMENTS—used for cost planning in Project Systems (environment 205)

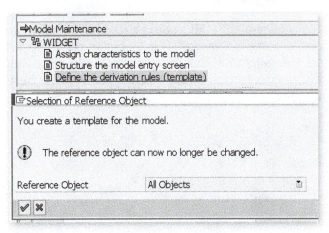

Figure 6.20: Creating the derivation rules

Select the reference object (environment) appropriate for the purpose of the cost estimation. Once the reference object is selected and the derivation rules have been saved, the reference object cannot be changed.

One special feature of the derivation rule templates is that the characteristics that are assigned to the model (see Section 6.3) are accessible as special functions available only for the current model. When looking at the function lists when maintaining formulas and methods, these use the name of the characteristic. Functions associated with numeric characteristics can be used in formulas and activation methods. Characteristics with the data type **CHAR** can be used for activation. Depending on how the characteristic was created, these can also be used in object determination. See Section 6.3.2 for a description of how characteristics are defined so they can be used in object determination.

The following columns are used in the Easy Cost Planning environments:

- ▶ TYPE—defines the cost item type in the resulting cost estimate, or a special row type such as a comment or reusable calculation.

- ▶ DESCRIPTION—is the description of the row. Normally this describes the object defined in Object Determination.

- ▶ OBJECT—is the object used for assigning cost to the cost estimate item. The types of objects that are allowed to be used in this column depend on the row type.

- ▶ QUANTITY—is the formula for calculating the quantity of the object used in the calculation of the item cost.

- ▶ UNIT—is the unit of measure associated with the quantity. This is the unit of measure assigned to the object in Object Determination. This cannot be edited.

- ▶ ACTIVATION—is the method used for determining if the item is to be included in the cost estimate.

- ▶ PRICE—is the price per unit of measure that is assigned to a variable costing item.

The means of maintaining individual rows for the rules derivation is identical to the method used for templates using transaction CPT1 and CPT2. There are several more row types available than for any other template environment. With the exception of comment rows and calculation rows, the allocation determined by an individual row results in one or more items on the Easy Cost Planning cost estimate.

6.5.1 Comment row

As in other types of templates, the comment row is used to document the actions of the template. Only the DESCRIPTION cell can be used for data entry. Comments can be up to 30 characters in length. However, a long description is possible by double clicking in the DESCRIPTION cell, and longer comments can be stored. Liberal use of comments is recommended because costing models can become very complex. Comment rows do not become a part of the cost estimate.

6.5.2 Business process row

This is used for the allocation of business process quantities to the cost estimate. The DESCRIPTION, OBJECT, QUANTITY, and ACTIVATION columns are active for this row type. Standard functions for object determination are used, and if the result of the method includes multiple business processes, then a separate itemization line is generated for each business process in the cost estimate. When using a characteristic to define the business process, the Field Reference function used for this is assigned to field PRZNR of structure CKF_RES_TPL. The standard function for identifying a single business process in object determination is SenderProcess.

Business process allocations are assigned item category X on the cost estimate.

6.5.3 Cost center/activity type row

This is used for the allocation of cost center/activity type quantities to the cost estimate. The DESCRIPTION, OBJECT, QUANTITY, and ACTIVATION columns are active for this row type. Standard functions for object determination are used, and if the result of the method includes multiple cost centers and/or activity types, then a separate itemization line is generated for each cost center/activity type combination in the cost estimate. When using a characteristic to define the cost center, the Field Reference function used for this is assigned to field KOSTL of structure CKF_RES_TPL. The LSTAR field defines the activity type. The standard function for specifying a single cost center is SenderCostCenter, and the standard function for a single activity type is SenderActivityType.

Item category E is used for internal activity allocations from cost centers and activity types.

6.5.4 Calculation row (business processes)

This is a calculation row using functions associated with business process type data. The Description, Object, Quantity, and Activation columns are active for this row type. The row object is the ID for the calculation that can be referenced in formulas for other rows. This particular row type has access to functions that are specific to business processes. See Section 2.6.3 for a more detailed description of calculation rows.

6.5.5 Calculation row (cost center/activity types)

This is a calculation row using functions associated with cost center/activity type data. The Description, Object, Quantity, and Activation columns are active for this row type. The row object is the ID for the calculation that can be referenced in formulas for other rows. This particular row type has access to functions that are specific to cost centers and activity types. See Section 2.6.3 for a more detailed description of calculation rows.

6.5.6 Costing model row

Subtemplates are not available for Easy Cost Planning because there is no independent means of creating the templates for the ECP application environments without creating a costing model with CKCM. This row type enables access to another costing model in a similar manner to how a subtemplate is used. The Description, Object, and Activation columns are active for this row type. Quantity calculations are not possible for costing models. Cost model IDs can be assigned to model characteristics. The cost model characteristic needs to be assigned to field MODEL of structure CKF_RES_TPL. The function to specify the model in object determination is COSTING_MODEL.

Each costing model is assigned characteristics. If the same characteristic is used in the main model and the costing model defined for this row type, then it will have the same value in both, and if the value is changed in one model, it will also be changed in the other. Care should be taken when designing cost estimates with multi-level models to ensure that use of characteristics is consistent.

Cost model results use item category J on the resulting cost estimate. The quantity assigned to a costing model cannot be changed.

6.5.7 External activity row

External activities involve manufacturing at an outside location that is linked directly to internal manufacturing processes. This differs from sub-contracting, which is used for sending component materials to an outside manufacturer and returning a finished product. The DESCRIPTION, OBJECT, QUANTITY, and ACTIVATION columns are active for this row type. Four pieces of information are required to define the source of the external activity cost: plant, purchasing organization, purchasing information record, and a cost element to assign to the resulting cost. The field references for the characteristics should be assigned to structure CKF_RES_TPL and the following four fields:

► Plant—WERKS

► Purchasing organization—EKORG

► Purchasing information record—INFNR_F

► Cost element—KSTAR

The corresponding functions for object determination are

► Plant—Plant

► Purchasing organization—PurchasingOrganization

► Purchasing information record—
   INFO_RECORD_NUMBER_EXT_SERV

► Cost element—CostElement

Item category F is assigned to external processing costing items.

6.5.8 Subcontracting row

This row type provides access to subcontracting purchasing information records to include that cost in the cost estimate. The DESCRIPTION, OBJECT, QUANTITY, and ACTIVATION columns are active for this row type. Four pieces of information are required to define the source of the subcontracting cost: plant, purchasing organization, purchasing information record, and a cost element to assign to the resulting cost. The field references for the characteristics should be assigned to structure CKF_RES_TPL and the following four fields:

- ▶ Plant—WERKS
- ▶ Purchasing organization—EKORG
- ▶ Purchasing information record—INFNR
- ▶ Cost element—KSTAR

The corresponding functions for object determination are:

- ▶ Plant—Plant
- ▶ Purchasing organization—PurchasingOrganization
- ▶ Purchasing information record—INFO_RECORD_NUMBER
- ▶ Cost element—CostElement

Item category L is assigned to subcontracting costing items.

6.5.9   Material row

This row type enables a material with its corresponding cost to be included in the cost estimate. The DESCRIPTION, OBJECT, QUANTITY, and ACTIVATION columns are active for this row type. Material costs are plant dependent, so both plant and material number are required to define the object. If assigned to characteristics, the plant characteristic should reference CKF_RES_TPL field WERKS, and the material should reference field MATNR. The Plant function is used to identify the plant for object determination, and Material is used for the material.

Item category M is used for material cost items.

6.5.10 Service row

The service row is used to assign the cost of a service from the service master to the cost estimate. The DESCRIPTION, OBJECT, QUANTITY, and ACTIVATION columns are active for this row type. The field references for the characteristics should be assigned to structure `CKF_RES_TPL` and the following five fields:

- ▶ Service ID (activity number)—`ASNUM`
- ▶ Plant—`WERKS`
- ▶ Purchasing organization—`EKORG`
- ▶ Vendor—`LIFNR`
- ▶ Cost element—`KSTAR`

The corresponding functions for object determination are:

- ▶ Service ID—`ACTIVITY_NUMBER`
- ▶ Plant—`Plant`
- ▶ Purchasing organization—`PurchasingOrganization`
- ▶ Vendor—`Vendor`
- ▶ Cost element—`CostElement`

Item category N is assigned to service costing items.

6.5.11 Base planning object row

Like materials and their costs, a base planning object can also be assigned to the cost estimate. The DESCRIPTION, OBJECT, QUANTITY, and ACTIVATION columns are active for this row type. Base planning objects require the base planning object ID and a cost element. If using characteristics for object determination, the base planning object characteristic should be assigned to structure `CKF_RES_TPL` and field `EXTNR`. Cost element should be assigned to field `KSTAR`. `BASE_PLANNING_OBJECT` is the function used to specify the base planning object. Cost element is selected with function `CostElement`.

The item category for base planning objects is B.

6.5.12 Text item row

Text items have no costs associated with them. However, they can be useful to provide comments in the resulting cost estimate. The DESCRIPTION cell is used to store the text, using up to 30 characters. Unlike comments in the comment row, text items show up in the final cost estimate itemization using item category T. The DESCRIPTION and ACTIVATION columns are active for this row type.

6.5.13 Variable item

Variable items are quite useful in that they enable the assignment of a specific cost to a line item. The DESCRIPTION, OBJECT, QUANTITY, ACTIVATION, and PRICE columns are active for this row type. Cost element and unit of measure are required to define the object for variable items. If using characteristics to define these, the cost element characteristic should be assigned to structure CKF_RES_TPL field KSTAR_V, and the unit of measure should be assigned to field MEEHT. The function for specifying the cost element is Cost_Element_Variable_Item, and the function for unit of measure is BASE_QUANTITY_UNIT.

The PRICE cell is a formula cell similar to the QUANTITY cell. Formulas that include numeric and currency data type characteristics can be used to define the price. The price defined is for one unit of measure. Characteristics defined with the **CURR** data type have a currency assigned to them.

The item category for variable items is V.

6.6   Create a cost estimate

Transaction CKECP is used for creating ad hoc cost estimates. These cost estimates can be based on costing models defined with transaction CKCM, or they can be manually defined in a similar fashion to the way unit cost estimates and base planning objects are defined, or there can be a combination of costing model and manually entered costing items. This section concentrates on the use of the templates defined in the costing model to generate the individual line items of the cost estimate.

The initial window of CKECP has tabs which contain worklists for the cost models and cost estimates that are actively being used. Figure 6.21 shows the initial CREATE WITH PLANNING FORMS tab that contains a list of planning forms (costing models) normally used for defining the cost estimates.

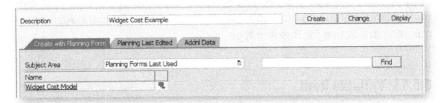

Figure 6.21: CKECP planning forms

Normally, only the most recently used planning forms are displayed, but any defined costing model can be selected. Click on the planning form name to use that model as the basis of the cost estimate. If a model is chosen, the focus changes to the ADDNL DATA tab to enter necessary costing variant parameters for the cost estimate (see Figure 6.22).

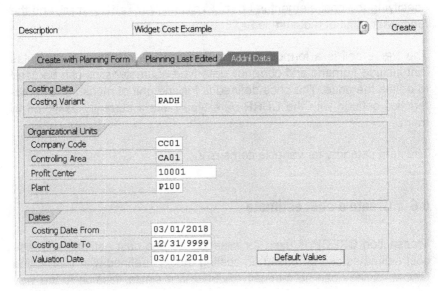

Figure 6.22: CKECP cost estimate data

Selecting a planning form on this tab is only required when creating a new cost estimate. Even for new cost estimates, this step can be by-passed. Planning forms can be selected from the cost estimate window. If no planning form is selected, cost items can also be directly entered in the cost estimate, similar to the way unit cost estimates are created.

Once cost estimates have been created, the PLANNING LAST EDITED tab is displayed to show the most recent cost estimates. This provides a shortcut for selecting a specific cost estimate to review or update. Click on the underlined description (see Figure 6.23) to go to that particular cost estimate. If the cost estimate in question does not appear on the list, it can be found using the dropdown list for DESCRIPTION at the top of the window.

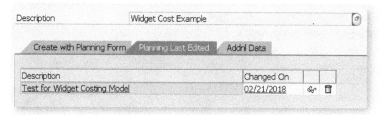

Figure 6.23: CKECP previous cost estimates

If an existing cost estimate is selected, the focus switches directly to the cost estimate window. That cost estimate, along with the saved charac-teristics used to define it, are then displayed. However, for new cost es-timates, costing parameters in the ADDNL DATA tab must be entered be-fore moving to the cost estimate window. If alternative ad hoc costing variants have been configured, one of them can be selected in this win-dow. PADH is the one delivered by SAP for use in ad hoc costing. Com-pany code, profit center and plant are entered in the ORGANIZATIONAL UNITS section. Finally, the costing dates need to be filled in.

Click on Create to create a new cost estimate. Click on Change to edit an existing cost estimate or Display to display a saved cost estimate.

6.6.1 Entering the characteristics

If a planning form has been selected, the data entry screen for that cost-ing model is displayed along with an empty costing structure. The win-dow is divided into two parts. The costing structure is displayed on the left and the data entry screen is on the right. Figure 6.24 shows the emp-ty cost estimate. Begin filling in the values for the model characteristics. If the F4 button has been enabled in the model, it can be used to select a specific object such as a material by using search windows particular to that object. Characteristics that have validation values assigned to them have a ▽ button which must be used to select one of the specific values assigned to that characteristic. The DANGEROUS GOODS INDICATOR in Figure 6.24 is an example of one of these characteristics.

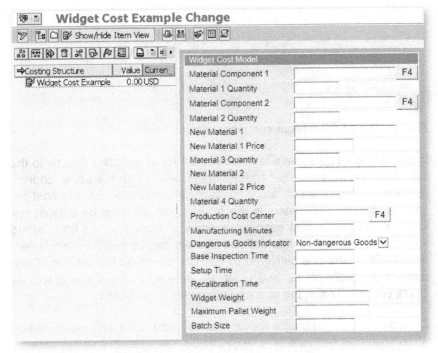

Figure 6.24: CKECP initial entry of characteristics

At the bottom of the data entry screen are two additional items associat-ed with the cost estimate. A description of the use of the cost estimate can be entered in the NOTE field (see Figure 6.25). This helps identify the reason for the cost estimate.

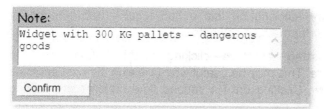

Figure 6.25: CKECP note and confirmation button

Once all the characteristics have been entered, click on the Confirm button or press the [Enter] key to generate the cost estimate. The result is shown in Figure 6.26. The COSTING STRUCTURE side of the window displays the details of the costs as determined by the characteristics entered on the right.

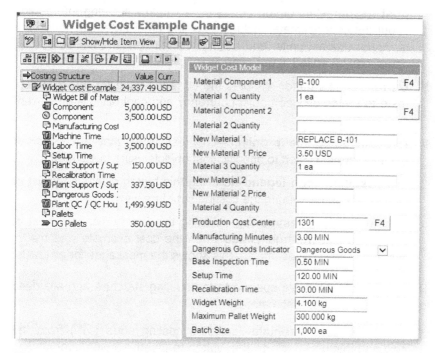

Figure 6.26: CKECP costing structure and characteristics

Two sets of buttons are used for manipulating and displaying additional information about the cost estimate. The top row of buttons applies to all areas of the cost estimate, including the itemization view window. These buttons are as follows:

- ⌦ **Change/display**—clicking on this button toggles between modify and display only for the cost estimate.

- ⌦ **Show/hide costing structure**—clicking on this button hides the costing structure. This may be useful when viewing the cost estimate itemization view. Clicking on it a second time restores the costing structure.

- ⌂ **Show/hide worklists**—a worklist of costing models can be displayed below the costing structure. Click on this button to display a list of models to use for cost estimates.

- ⌦ Show/Hide Item View **Show/hide itemization**—clicking on this button toggles between a display of the itemization view below the data entry screen, or no display. This is covered in Section 6.6.2.

- ⌦ **Cost header**—this button brings up a window showing information about the cost estimate, including costing data, dates, valuation data, organizational units, and history. Certain fields, such as costing dates, can be edited in this window.

- ⌦ **Currency**—this button enables the currency used for the cost estimate to switch between object currency and controlling area currency.

- ⌦ **Account assignment object**—cost estimates that are used for planning are assigned to specific cost objects using this button.

- ⌦ **Cost estimate icon legend**—clicking this button displays the list of icons that can be seen in the costing structure view.

- ⌦ **Cost estimate message log**—clicking this button displays a list of messages that were generated when the cost estimate was made. For multi-level cost estimates, this shows the messages for all levels.

The following buttons are specific to the costing structure and are used to manipulate the cost estimate:

- ⌦ **Subdivide cost estimate**—select a costing node (⌦) from the costing structure. Click on this button to insert a lower level costing node. The system prompts for a name, a costing lot size, and a unit of measure to assign to the costing node. The focus of the data entry window and the itemization view changes to this costing level. Because no model has been assigned to this costing node, the Choose Planning Form button is displayed on the data entry window so that the proper planning form can be selected for that level of the cost. This is a very powerful tool in that it provides a flexible way of building up a high-level cost using multiple levels of individual components.

Revaluate—click on this button to revalue the entire costing structure based on the changes that have been made to it.

Rename cost estimate—this button renames the current cost estimate so that it can be saved with a different name.

Delete cost estimate—use this button to delete the cost estimate.

Remove planning form—this button disassociates the planning form from a specific costing node in the costing structure. This makes it possible to select an alternative planning form for that costing level. Any cost estimate and characteristic values associated with that costing node are then deleted from the cost estimate.

Document flow—click on this button to see the document flow for the cost estimate used in a planning environment.

Close—this button is used to lock the cost estimate from further changes. Click on the button again to allow for changes.

Show/hide costing structure—clicking on this button toggles between showing the lower levels of the selected costing node or just the rolled-up costs for the costing node.

6.6.2 Itemization section

Click on the Show/Hide Item View to bring up the itemization window (see Figure 6.27). Not only does this display the cost estimate in an ALV grid, it also enables the values in the cost estimate to be edited. Editing functionality for the cost estimate is similar to that of unit costing (transaction CKUC) and base planning object costing (transactions KKE1 and KKE2). The display is in ALV grid format, enabling export to spreadsheets as well as the creation of report layouts to show the desired fields on the report.

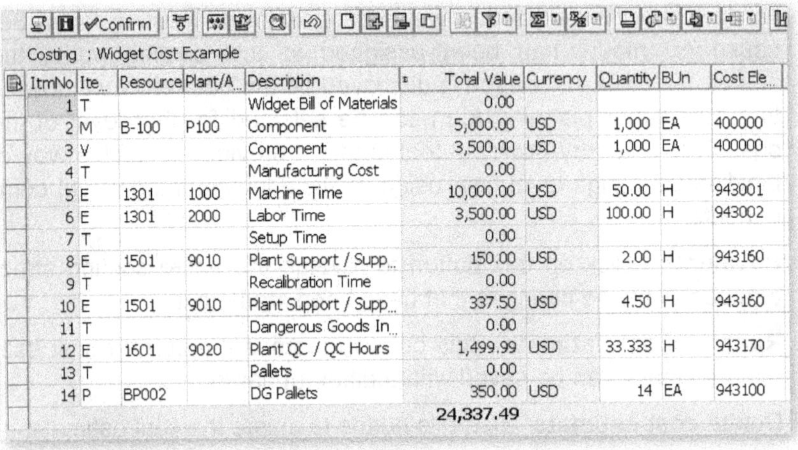

ItmNo	Ite	Resource	Plant/A	Description	Total Value	Currency	Quantity	BUn	Cost Ele
1	T			Widget Bill of Materials	0.00				
2	M	B-100	P100	Component	5,000.00	USD	1,000	EA	400000
3	V			Component	3,500.00	USD	1,000	EA	400000
4	T			Manufacturing Cost	0.00				
5	E	1301	1000	Machine Time	10,000.00	USD	50.00	H	943001
6	E	1301	2000	Labor Time	3,500.00	USD	100.00	H	943002
7	T			Setup Time	0.00				
8	E	1501	9010	Plant Support / Supp...	150.00	USD	2.00	H	943160
9	T			Recalibration Time	0.00				
10	E	1501	9010	Plant Support / Supp...	337.50	USD	4.50	H	943160
11	T			Dangerous Goods In...	0.00				
12	E	1601	9020	Plant QC / QC Hours	1,499.99	USD	33.333	H	943170
13	T			Pallets	0.00				
14	P	BP002		DG Pallets	350.00	USD	14	EA	943100
					24,337.49				

Costing : Widget Cost Example

Figure 6.27: CKECP itemization window

As in standard cost estimates, the itemization window displays the detailed lines of the selected costing node of the costing structure. If a planning form was used for creating the cost estimate, then the values of the itemization are determined by the template assigned to the selected costing model. However, the resulting costs can be manually changed in the itemization window, and line items can be directly entered without having to use a planning form. This mimics what can be done with unit costing and base planning objects. There are several buttons which can be used to manipulate the itemization and display details about the itemization:

Cost estimate log—clicking this button displays the message log for the specific costing node represented by the itemization window.

Item information—select an item line and click on this button to get detailed information about the specific object.

✓Confirm **Confirm cost estimate**—after all changes have been made to the cost estimate, click on this button to save those changes.

Fill column—select the item lines. Then, select the cell to copy by clicking the left mouse button with the (Ctrl) key pressed. Click on the button to paste the contents of that cell into the other selected cells of that column.

Revaluate all items—click on this button to revalue all lines in the itemization after making changes.

- **Revaluate selected items**—first select specific lines from the itemization that have been changed. Then click on this button to revalue those items, but no other items in the cost estimate.

- **Explode base planning object**—select a base planning object (item category B) from the cost estimate. Click on this button to replace the base planning object line with the individual line items from the base planning object.

- **Change/display costing lot size**—click on this button to see the costing lot size of this costing node. The lot size can be changed. This affects only the current costing node, and the costing structure should be revalued after making a change.

- **Detail display**—select a line from the itemization. Clicking this button brings up a window showing the value of all possible columns of the report for this line.

- **Undo changes**—click on this button to undo the recent typing in a field.

- **Append line**—click on this button to add a new line at the end of the itemization.

- **Insert line**—select a line and click on this button to insert an empty line before the selected line.

- **Delete line**—select a line and click on this button to delete that line from the itemization.

- **Duplicate row**—select a line and click on this button to duplicate the selected line.

In addition to the above functions, standard ALV grid buttons for manipulating layouts, filtering, totaling, subtotaling, and exporting data are also available.

The details of the cost estimate are divided into 6 sections. Each section has a text item included to describe the purpose of each section.

Bill of materials

The widget model allows for four different items to be assigned as components in the cost estimate. In effect, these form the BOM. The material lines of the cost estimate are shown in Figure 6.28, section ❶. Although four items are defined in the template (❷), only two material lines make up a part of the cost estimate. This is because only the MATERIAL COMPONENT 1 and NEW MATERIAL 1 characteristics are assigned values (❸). The activation cells for these rows determine whether the material lines show up in the cost estimate. The activation method for the first material row is `ECP-MATERIAL-1 <> ''`. The second material activation method uses the ECP-MATERIAL-2 characteristic for activation. Since characteristic ECP-MATERIAL-1 has a value, it becomes a part of the cost estimate. ECP-MATERIAL-2 has no value, and therefore is not a part of the cost estimate. The same is true of the two speculative materials (characteristics ECP-NEW-MAT-1 and ECP-NEW-MAT-2). Because the characteristic ECP-NEW-MAT-1 has a value, it becomes a part of the cost estimate. The activation method for that row is `ECP-NEW-MAT-1 <> ''`.

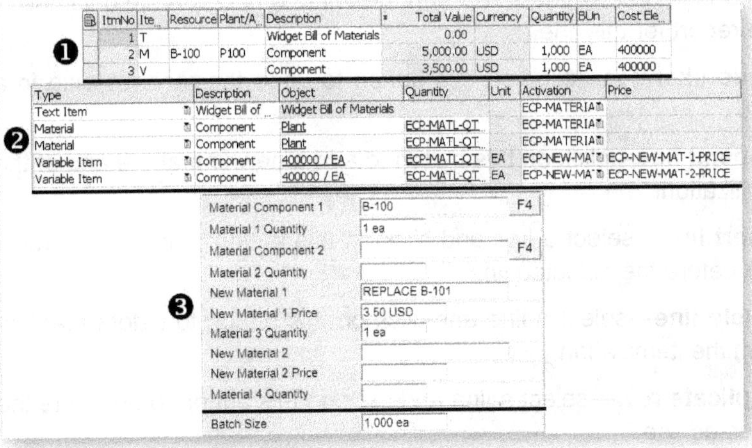

Figure 6.28: BOM cost determination

Item 1 of the cost estimate is a text item to describe this section of the cost estimate. Item 2 has category M from the Material template row type associated with it. This is required in order to be a valid material in the system, and it is defined in the object determination cell. The method used is `Plant = 'P100' AND MATERIAL_NUMBER IN ECP-MATERIAL-1`. The material number comes from the value entered into characteristic ECP-MATERIAL-1. This material is extended to plant P100. If no valid material/plant combination is selected, then an error shows in the resulting cost estimate and no line is displayed. In our example, material *B-100* was entered and shows up in the cost estimate. The quantity formula for this line takes the value assigned to MATERIAL

QUANTITY 1 (characteristic ECP-MATL-QTY-1) and multiplies this by the batch size in characteristic ECP-BATCH-SIZE. This gives the value of 1,000 that shows up in line 2 of the cost estimate. The price of the material is used in the calculation of the total cost.

Item 3 of the cost estimate has item category V, which indicates that it is determined from a Variable Item row in the template. The object determination uses `Cost_Element_Variable_Item = '400000' AND BASE_QUANTITY_UNIT = 'EA'`. In this case, the values are directly specified. The quantity formula is the same as for the material lines. In this case, it is `ECP-MATL-QTY-3 * ECP-BATCH-SIZE`. For material lines, the cost comes from the material cost in the material master. Variable items do not have a costing source, and PRICE cell is used for defining the cost. This uses the value assigned to characteristic ECP-NEW-MATL-1-PRICE.

Manufacturing costs

The manufacturing costs in a standard cost estimate are derived from activity types planned in a cost center associated with the work center of the route. Easy Cost Planning does not have access to routes and recipes. The steps used for determining costs associated with a route operation are created in the template (❷). As part of the requirements for this cost model, an alternative method of manufacturing can be used that is different to the one used for the standard materials. Therefore, the production cost center can be entered as a characteristic. The manufacturing time is also a characteristic, so changes can be made to model how the costs would be affected by speeding up or slowing down the manufacturing process. The relevant characteristics for the calculations are in section ❸ of Figure 6.29.

❶	4 T			Manufacturing Cost		0.00			
	5 E	1301	1000	Machine Time		10,000.00 USD	50.00	H	943001
	6 E	1301	2000	Labor Time		3,500.00 USD	100.00	H	943002

	Type	Description	Object	Quantity	Unit	Activation
❷	Text Item	Manufacturing	Manufacturing Cost			ECP-PROD-CC
	Cost Center/Activity Type	Machine Time	SenderCostCenter	ECP-BATCH-SI		ECP-PROD-CC
	Cost Center/Activity Type	Labor Time	SenderCostCenter	ECP-BATCH-SI		ECP-PROD-CC

	Production Cost Center	1301	F4
❸	Manufacturing Minutes	3.00 MIN	
	Batch Size	1.000 ea	

Figure 6.29: Manufacturing cost determination

There are two activity types that are relevant to the cost estimate. These are 1000 (machine cost) and 2000 (labor cost). The activation method for both items is `ECP-PROD-CCTR <> ''`. This method is in the ACTIVATION column in section ❷. If the cost center is not entered, then no manufacturing costs are included in the cost estimate. The object determination method is `SenderCostCenter IN ECP-PROD-CCTR AND SenderActivtyType = '1000'` for the machine time line. Activity type 2000 is assigned to `SenderActivityType` for the labor line. The time calculation uses a formula that takes the batch size in characteristic ECP-BATCH-SIZE and multiplies it by the manufacturing minutes in ECP-MFG-TIME. This is then divided by 60 to convert it to hours. The labor line item multiples that by 2 to account for 2 people running the machine. Section ❶ shows the result in the cost estimate.

Setup and recalibration costs

These two sections utilize the same cost center/activity type for the allocation of the costs. The setup and recalibration costs each have their own text lines to make them stand out on the cost estimate. There is a specific characteristic each for setup time and recalibration time. These times are used to control the activation in the template rows of section ❷ of Figure 6.30. The activation method for the setup items is `ECP-SETUP-TIME <> '0'`, and the method for the recalibration items is `ECP-RECAL-TIME <> '0'`.

❶	7 T			Setup Time	0.00				
	8 E	1501	9010	Plant Support / Supp...	150.00	USD	2.00	H	943160
	9 T			Recalibration Time	0.00				
	10 E	1501	9010	Plant Support / Supp...	337.50	USD	4.50	H	943160

	Type	Description	Object	Quantity	Unit	Activation
	Text Item	Setup Time	Setup Time			ECP-SETUP-T.▣
❷	Cost Center/Activity Type	Plant Support /...	1501 / 9010	ECP-SETUP-TI...	H	ECP-SETUP-T.▣
	Text Item	Recalibration Ti...	Recalibration Time			ECP-RECAL-TI▣
	Cost Center/Activity Type	Plant Support /...	1501 / 9010	Floor((ECP-B...	H	ECP-RECAL-TI▣

❸	Setup Time	120.00 MIN
	Recalibration Time	30.00 MIN
	Batch Size	1,000 ea

Figure 6.30: Setup and recalibration cost determination

Object determination for both of these items is the same (cost center 1501, activity type 9010). The setup time is a fixed quantity regardless of batch size. Its formula is `ECP-SETUP-TIME / 60` to convert the minutes to hours used by the activity type. The entered batch size is not included in the calculation. The recalibration formula, first defined in Chapter 2, is more complex because it must take into account that recalibration occurs after every 100 widgets that are manufactured. The formula for this is `Floor( ( ECP-BATCH-SIZE - 100 ) / 100 ) * ECP-RECAL-TIME / 60`. Because the same setup and recalibration times were used as in the original production scenario (❸), the values assigned to this in the cost estimate (❶) should match what was found in the standard cost estimate for widget A-100 in Chapter 2.

Inspection costs

Looking back to the original costing scenario from Chapter 2, the time associated with inspection depends on two things: the dangerous goods indicator and the number of components. First, each component is inspected before it is used in production, and it takes twice as long to inspect widget components that are designated as dangerous goods. Figure 6.31 shows the relevant items in the cost estimate (❶), the template (❷), and the characteristic entry window (❸). Even though there are four lines for inspection in the template, only two are shown in the cost estimate. The first line is the text item (category T), indicating that it is a "dangerous goods inspection". This text item is selected because the dangerous goods indicator characteristic (ECP-DG-INDICATOR) is chosen. The VALUES tab of the characteristic definition has the two selections defined (see Section 6.3), and a dropdown window was used to get the value. The activation for the text line checks to see if the inspection time is not 0 and the dangerous goods indicator is selected. This is represented by `ECP-INSP-TIME <> '0' AND ECP-DG-INDICATOR = 'X'`.

11	T			Dangerous Goods In	0.00			
12	E	1601	9020	Plant QC / QC Hours	1,499.99	USD	33.333 H	943170

Type	Description	Object	Quantity	Unit	Activation
Text Item	Non Dangerou	Non Dangerous Goods			ECP-INSP-TIM
Cost Center/Activity Type	Plant QC / QC	1601 / 9020	ECP-BATCH-SI	H	ECP-INSP-TIM
Text Item	Dangerous Go	Dangerous Goods Ins			ECP-INSP-TIM
Cost Center/Activity Type	Plant QC / QC	1601 / 9020	ECP-BATCH-SI	H	ECP-INSP-TIM

Material Component 1	B-100 F4
Material 1 Quantity	1 ea
Material Component 2	F4
Material 2 Quantity	
New Material 1	REPLACE B-101
New Material 1 Price	3.50 USD
Material 3 Quantity	1 ea
New Material 2	
New Material 2 Price	
Material 4 Quantity	

Dangerous Goods Indicator	Dangerous Goods
Base Inspection Time	0.50 MIN
Batch Size	1,000 ea

Figure 6.31: Inspection cost determination

The actual cost item for the cost estimate uses the same method for activation. Inspection is represented by activity type 9020 in cost center 1601. Note that this is the same for both the non-dangerous goods inspection and the dangerous goods inspection, so the object determination cell is the same for both template rows. The activation is different, which means only the dangerous goods template rows become part of this cost estimate. The formula for calculating the activity quantity is ECP-BATCH-SIZE * (ECP-MATL-QTY-1 + ECP-MATL-QTY-2 + ECP-MATL-QTY-3 + ECP-MATL-QTY-4) * ECP-INSP-TIME / 60 * 2. The batch size represents the quantity used for the cost calculation. Because inspection occurs for all components, the quantities for all components must be added up and then multiplied by the costing size. Values have been assigned to two of the component characteristics in section ❸: MATERIAL COMPONENT 1 and NEW MATERIAL 1. Therefore, the total components per produced widget is 2. The base inspection time is defined in minutes, and this must be divided by 60 to get the hours. The result is multiplied by 2, because our specification says that dangerous goods inspection takes twice as long as standard inspection. The resulting cost is the value of the 9020 activity type multiplied by the quantity determined in this formula.

Pallet costs

One purpose of the cost model is to determine the cost impact of adjusting the weight capacity of the pallets. The standard weight was 250 kg, but in this example 300 kg is used in the calculations (see ❸ in Figure 6.32). The standard pallet business processes, BP001 for non-dangerous goods and BP002 for dangerous goods, are used in the model (❷). Business process BP002 is selected because the dangerous goods indicator is set.

❶	13 T		Pallets		0.00				
	14 P	BP002	DG Pallets		350.00	USD	14 EA	943100
	Type		Description	Object	Quantity	Unit	Activation		
❷	Text Item		Pallets	Pallets					
	Business Process		Standard Pallets	BP001	Ceil(ECP-BAT	EA	ECP-DG-INDIC		
	Business Process		Standard Pallets	BP002	Ceil(ECP-BAT	EA	ECP-DG-INDIC		

Dangerous Goods Indicator	Dangerous Goods	∨
❸ Widget Weight	4.100 kg	
Maximum Pallet Weight	300.000 kg	
Batch Size	1,000 ea	

Figure 6.32: Pallet packing cost determination

The formula takes into account the batch size, the widget weight, and the maximum pallet weight to determine the number of pallets for the batch size (14 in section ❶). This formula is `Ceil( ECP-BATCH-SIZE / Floor( ECP-PALLET-WT / ECP-NEW-MAT-WT-1 ) )`. This emulates the pallet formula from the WDGTPACK subtemplate used in Chapter 2.

6.6.3 Reusing costing models

Multiple cost estimates can be generated using the same costing model. Existing cost estimates can be modified by updating the characteristics, or new cost estimates can be created from the same model. The purpose of the costing model is to provide a consistent set of parameters which can be used to generate and compare costs.

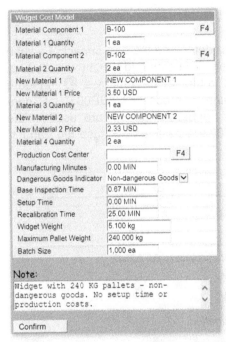

Figure 6.33: Second cost estimate characteristics

Figure 6.33 shows the data entry screen using the same model with different characteristics filled in. All four BOM items were entered, production cost center was left blank, and setup time was set to 0. Different values were assigned to various other characteristics.

ItmNo	Ite	Resource	Plant/A	Description		Total Value	Currency	Quantity	BUn	Cost Ele
1	T			Widget Bill of Materials		0.00				
2	M	B-100	P100	Component		5,000.00	USD	1,000	EA	400000
3	V			Component		3,500.00	USD	1,000	EA	400000
4	T			Manufacturing Cost		0.00				
5	E	1301	1000	Machine Time		10,000.00	USD	50.00	H	943001
6	E	1301	2000	Labor Time		3,500.00	USD	100.00	H	943002
7	T			Setup Time		0.00				
8	E	1501	9010	Plant Support / Supp...		150.00	USD	2.00	H	943160
9	T			Recalibration Time		0.00				
10	E	1501	9010	Plant Support / Supp...		337.50	USD	4.50	H	943160
11	T			Dangerous Goods In...		0.00				
12	E	1601	9020	Plant QC / QC Hours		1,499.99	USD	33.333	H	943170
13	T			Pallets		0.00				
14	P	BP002		DG Pallets		350.00	USD	14	EA	943100
						24,337.49				

Costing : Widget Cost Example

Figure 6.34: First cost estimate itemization

The original cost estimate for this chapter is displayed in Figure 6.34.

ItmNo	Ite	Resource	Plant/A	Description		Total Value	Currency	Quantity	BUn	Cost Ele
1	T			Widget Bill of Materials		0.00				
2	M	B-100	P100	Component		5,000.00	USD	1,000	EA	400000
3	M	B-102	P100	Component		0.20	USD	2,000	EA	400000
4	V			Component		3,500.00	USD	1,000	EA	400000
5	V			Component		4,660.00	USD	2,000	EA	400000
6	T			Recalibration Time		0.00				
7	E	1501	9010	Plant Support / Supp..		281.25	USD	3.75	H	943160
8	T			Non Dangerous Goo..		0.00				
9	E	1601	9020	Plant QC / QC Hours		3,015.00	USD	67.00	H	943170
10	T			Pallets		0.00				
11	P	BP001		Standard Pallets		220.00	USD	22	EA	943100
						16,676.45				

Costing : Widget Cost Example

Figure 6.35: Second cost estimate itemization

Figure 6.35 shows the effects of having made changes to the character-istics entries. In comparing the two results, several differences can be seen. Four components are now included instead of the original two. There is now no manufacturing section because the cost center was left blank in the data entry screen. There is no setup time in the second cost estimate, because the setup time was set to 0 when entering the charac-teristics. The non-dangerous goods inspection is now used due to the selection of the DANGEROUS GOODS INDICATOR. The inspection time is greater due to the number of components in the BOM section. Finally, because NON-DANGEROUS GOODS was selected for the cost estimate, business process BP001 was used for the pallets instead of BP002. The resulting cost estimate, as well as the costing result, can be very differ-ent depending on how the templates are defined and how the character-istics are entered.

7 Appendix

7.1 Template applications

Template applications are a method of grouping together like environments. Applications are used when filtering the environments displayed when maintaining template functions with transaction CTU6. A list of applications is shown in Table 7.1.

Application	Description
COB	Cost Objects
CPI	Formula Planning
ECP	Easy Cost Planning
ISB	Financial Objects
PAC	Costing Based Profitability Analysis
PCA	Profit Center Planning
SBP	Activity Assignments
SKI	Actual Statistical Key Figures
SOP	Transfer Sales and Operation Planning

Table 7.1: Template applications

7.2 Environments and sub-environments

Table 7.2 shows the main template environments and their available sub-environments.

Env	Description	Applic	Sub-environments
001	Cost estimate/ production orders	COB	101 102 103 104 105 107 115 116 125
002	Reference and simulation costing	COB	101 106 107 115 125
003	Cost estimate w/o quantity str.	COB	101 102 103 106 107 115 125

Env	Description	Applic	Sub-environments
004	Network	COB	101 107 108 115 125
005	WBS element	COB	101 106 107 109 115 125
006	General cost objects/ CO hierarchy	COB	101 106 107 112 115 125
007	Internal order	COB	101 106 107 110 115 125
008	Sales order	COB	101 103 104 105 106 107 111 115 125
009	Process order	COB	101 102 103 104 105 107 115 116 125
010	Product cost collector	COB	101 103 107 115 125 126
011	Service order	COB	101 102 103 107 114 115 125
012	CO production order	COB	101 103 106 107 113 115 125
200	ECP: general costing characteristic	ECP	101 106 107 115 125 299
205	ECP: PSP-Element	ECP	101 106 107 109 115 125 299
206	ECP: gen.cost object/cst obj hier.	ECP	101 106 107 112 115 125 299
207	ECP: internal order	ECP	101 106 107 110 115 125 299
208	ECP: customer order	ECP	101 103 104 105 106 107 111 115 125 299
214	ECP: message	ECP	101 107 115 125 299
215	ECP: appropriation request	ECP	101 106 107 115 125 299
BAC	Accounts	ISB	101 107 125 BFO BPA
BCD	Money mrkt, forex, derivatives	ISB	101 107 125 BFO
BKK	Bank customer accounts	ISB	101 107 125 BFO BPA

Env	Description	Applic	Sub-environments
BLN	Loans	ISB	101 107 125 BFO BPA
BPP	Business process planning	CPI	107 115 120 121 128
BSO	Security orders	ISB	101 107 125 BFO BST
BSS	Securities positions	ISB	101 107 125 BFO BST
BST	Security class data	ISB	BST
BSV	Services	ISB	101 107 125 BFO BPA
BVT	Variable transaction	ISB	101 107 125 BFO BPA
CPD	Activity-dep. cost center planning	CPI	107 115 120 121 122 123 124 CPI
CPI	Activity-indep. cost ctr planning	CPI	107 115 120 121 122 124 EXP
PAC	Costing-based profitability analysis	PAC	101 107 115 125
PCA	Profit center planning	PCA	107 115 121 130 131 132
SBP	Business processes	SBP	101 107 115 125 128 129
SCD	Cost centers/Activity types	SBP	101 107 115 122 123 125 129
SCI	Cost centers	SBP	101 107 115 122 125 129
SKD	Statistical key figure act. dep.	SKI	107 115 120 121 122 123
SKI	Statistical key figure act. indep.	SKI	107 115 120 121 122
SOP	Transfer sales and operations plan	SOP	101 103 107 115 125

Table 7.2: Environments and associated sub-environments

Table 7.3 shows the sub-environments and in which environments they are used.

Sub	Description	Environments
000	Test environment	
101	Sender processes	001 002 003 004 005 006 007 008 009 010 011 012 200 205 206 207 208 214 215 BAC BCD BKK BLN BSO BSS BSV BVT PAC SBP SCD SCI SOP
102	Order data	001 003 009 011
103	Materials	001 003 008 009 010 011 012 208 SOP
104	Bill of material	001 008 009 208
105	Routing	001 008 009 208
106	Unit costing	002 003 005 006 007 008 012 200 205 206 207 208 215
107	General data	001 002 003 004 005 006 007 008 009 010 011 012 200 205 206 207 208 214 215 BAC BCD BKK BLN BPP BSO BSS BSV BVT CPD CPI PAC PCA SBP SCD SCI SKD SKI SOP
108	Network	004
109	WBS element	005 205
110	Internal order	007 207
111	Sales order	008 208
112	General cost obj/hierarchy	006 206
113	CO production order	012
114	Service order	011

Sub	Description	Environments
115	Mathematical functions	001 002 003 004 005 006 007 008 009 010 011 012 200 205 206 207 208 214 215 BPP CPD CPI PAC PCA SBP SCD SCI SKD SKI SOP
116	Production campaign	001 009
120	Cost elements	BPP CPD CPI SKD SKI
121	Statistical key figures	BPP CPD CPI PCA SKD SKI
122	Receiver cost centers	CPD CPI SCD SCI SKD SKI
123	Receiver activity types	CPD SCD SKD
124	Resources	CPD CPI
125	Send CCTR/Acty Type	001 002 003 004 005 006 007 008 009 010 011 012 200 205 206 207 208 214 215 BAC BCD BKK BLN BSO BSS BSV BVT PAC SBP SCD SCI SOP
126	Sub-env.: Prod. cost collector	010
128	Business processes	BPP SBP
129	Activity allocation	SBP SCD SCI
130	Accounts	PCA
131	Profit center	PCA
132	Movement data for profit center	PCA
299	ECP: costing characteristic (sub)	200 205 206 207 208 214 215
BFO	Financial objects	BAC BCD BKK BLN BSO BSS BSV BVT
BPA	Business partner	BAC BKK BLN BSV BVT
BST	Security class data	BSO BSS
EXP	Express planning	CPI

Table 7.3: Sub-environments and associated environments

7.3 Tables and structures by environment

Table COTPLTABLE contains the list of tables and structures and the environments to which they are available. This list is static and is duplicated in Table 7.4.

Env	Table/Structure	Description
101	CBPRF	Sender process
102	AFKO	Order header
102	AFRU	Order confirmations
102	AUFK	Order master data
103	CKSONDERBESCHAFFUNG	Special procurement info
103	MARA	Material
103	MARC	Material by plant
104	MSEG	Material document
104	RESBD	BOM item/material component
105	AFVGD	Operation/network activity
106	KHS1	Unit costing
106	KIS1	Costing item
107	ABC_CON	General data
107	CKI_TCK05	Valuation variants
107	RKWTP	Template allocation
107	SYST	System data
108	AFKO	Order header
108	AFVGD	Operation/network activity
108	AUFK	Order master data
108	RESBD	BOM item/material component
109	PRPS	WBS element
110	AUFK	Order master data
111	AFKO	Order header
111	VBAK	Sales order header
111	VBAP	Sales order item
112	CKPH	General cost object

Env	Table/Structure	Description
113	AUFK	Order master data
116	PCMPB	Production campaign item
121	CSKAF	Cost elements
121	TKA03	Statistical key figures
122	CSKS	Cost centers
122	TKA09	Version
123	CSSL	Cost centers/activity types
124	CSKR_EXT	Resources
125	CSSL_TPL	Cost center/activity type
128	RCBPR	Receiver process
128	TKA09	Version
130	PCA_ACCOUNT	Accounts
131	CEPC	Profit center
132	T001	Company code
132	TKA09	Version
215	CKF_APPREQUEST_VARIANT	Appropriation request
299	CKF_RES_TPL	ECP: Resources
BAC	JBDKKON	Account master
BCD	VTBFHA	Financial transaction
BFO	JBDOBJ1	Financial object - general
BFO	JBISTWF	Financial object - per. Values
BFO	JBTOBJ1	Financial object - STC part
BKK	BKK42	BCA Master data
BKK	BKKIT	BCA Transaction data
BLN	VDARL	Loan master
BLN	VZZKOKO	Conditions header - loans
BPA	BP1010	Business partner-cred.rating
BSO	VWBEKI	Security order trans. header
BSO	VWBEPI	Security transaction data
BSO	VWPDEPO	Securities account position
BSS	JBDBSTD	Securities position

219

Env	Table/Structure	Description
BSS	VWPDEPO	Securities account position
BST	VWPAKTI	Security master
BST	VWPANLA	Asset master
BST	VWPANLE	Interest-bearing secur. Master
BST	VWPTERM	Warrants master
BSV	JBDSERV	Services
BVT	JBDVTMD	Variable transaction master
PAC	COPAOBJ	Profitability segment
SOP	KSOP	Plan requirements
SOP	PLAF	Planned order
SOP	SAUF	SOP Orders

Table 7.4: Environment table assignment

7.4   Row types

Row types are assigned by application. These assignments are defined in Table COTPLDEFLINETYP. and are listed here in Table 7.5. Each of the environments assigned to the application has access to that application's row types.

Application	Row Types
COB	Comment row
COB	Business process
COB	Subtemplate
COB	Cost center/activity type
COB	Calculation row (business process)
COB	Calculation row (cost center/activity type)
CPI	Comment row
CPI	Subtemplate
CPI	Statistical key figure
CPI	Calculation row

Application	Row Types
CPI	Cost element
CPI	Resource
ECP	Comment row
ECP	Business process
ECP	Cost center/activity type
ECP	Calculation row (business process)
ECP	Calculation row (cost center/activity type)
ECP	Costing model
ECP	External activity
ECP	Subcontracting
ECP	Material
ECP	Service
ECP	Base planning object
ECP	Text item
ECP	Variable item
ISB	Comment row
ISB	Business process
ISB	Subtemplate
ISB	Cost center/activity type
ISB	Calculation row (business process)
ISB	Calculation row (cost center/activity type)
PAC	Comment row
PAC	Business process
PAC	Subtemplate
PAC	Cost center/activity type
PAC	Calculation row (business process)
PAC	Calculation row (cost center/activity type)
PCA	Comment row
PCA	Subtemplate
PCA	Statistical key figure
PCA	Calculation row (account)
PCA	P&l account

Application	Row Types
PCA	Balance sheet account
SBP	Comment row
SBP	Business process
SBP	Subtemplate
SBP	Cost center/activity type
SBP	Calculation row (business process)
SBP	Calculation row (cost center/activity type)
SKI	Comment row
SKI	Subtemplate
SKI	Statistical key figure
SKI	Calculation row
SOP	Comment row
SOP	Business process
SOP	Subtemplate
SOP	Cost center/activity type
SOP	Calculation row (business process)
SOP	Calculation row (cost center/activity type)

Table 7.5: Template rows by application

Refer to Table 7.1 for a list of applications and to Table 7.2 for the environments associated with each application.

7.5 Column types

The column types used in templates are dependent on which main environment is used. Table 7.6 lists the columns by environment.

Environment	Column Types
001	Type | Description | Object | Unit | Plan quantity | Plan fix | Plan activation | Actual quantity | Actual fix | Actual activation | Actual allocation event
002	Type | Description | Object | Unit | Plan quantity | Plan activation

Environment	Column Types
003	Type | Description | Object | Unit | Plan quantity | Plan activation
004	Type | Description | Object | Unit | Plan quantity | Plan activation | Plan allocation event | Actual quantity | Actual activation | Actual allocation event
005	Type | Description | Object | Unit | Plan quantity | Plan activation | Plan allocation event | Actual quantity | Actual activation | Actual allocation event
006	Type | Description | Object | Unit | Plan quantity | Plan fix | Plan activation | Actual quantity | Actual fix | Actual activation | Actual allocation event
007	Type | Description | Object | Unit | Plan quantity | Plan fix | Plan activation | Actual quantity | Actual fix | Actual activation | Actual allocation event
008	Type | Description | Object | Unit | Plan quantity | Plan fix | Plan activation | Actual quantity | Actual fix | Actual activation | Actual allocation event
009	Type | Description | Object | Unit | Plan quantity | Plan fix | Plan activation | Actual quantity | Actual fix | Actual activation | Actual allocation event
010	Type | Description | Object | Unit | Plan quantity | Plan fix | Plan activation | Actual quantity | Actual fix | Actual activation | Actual allocation event
011	Type | Description | Object | Unit | Plan quantity | Plan fix | Plan activation | Actual quantity | Actual fix | Actual activation | Actual allocation event
012	Type | Description | Object | Unit | Plan quantity | Plan fix | Plan activation | Actual quantity | Actual fix | Actual activation | Actual allocation event
200	Type | Description | Object | Quantity | Unit | Activation | Price
205	Type | Description | Object | Quantity | Unit | Activation | Price

Environment	Column Types
206	Type | Description | Object | Quantity | Unit | Activation | Price
207	Type | Description | Object | Quantity | Unit | Activation | Price
208	Type | Description | Object | Quantity | Unit | Activation | Price
214	Type | Description | Object | Quantity | Unit | Activation | Price
215	Type | Description | Object | Quantity | Unit | Activation | Price
BAC	Type | Name | Object | Unit | Cumulated quantity | Cumulated activation | Periodic quantity | Periodic activation
BCD	Type | Name | Object | Unit | Cumulated quantity | Cumulated activation | Periodic quantity | Periodic activation
BKK	Type | Name | Object | Unit | Cumulated quantity | Cumulated activation | Periodic quantity | Periodic activation
BLN	Type | Name | Object | Unit | Cumulated quantity | Cumulated activation | Periodic quantity | Periodic activation
BPP	Type | Object | Description | Var, plan costs per acty. Unit per period | Fixed plan costs per period | Var. plan qty. per acty. Unit per period | Fixed plan qty. per period | Activation condition
BSO	Type | Name | Object | Unit | Cumulated quantity | Cumulated activation | Periodic quantity | Periodic activation
BSS	Type | Name | Object | Unit | Cumulated quantity | Cumulated activation | Periodic quantity | Periodic activation

Environment	Column Types
BST	Type | Name | Object | Unit | Cumulated quantity | Cumulated activation | Periodic quantity | Periodic activation
BSV	Type | Name | Object | Unit | Cumulated quantity | Cumulated activation | Periodic quantity | Periodic activation
BVT	Type | Name | Object | Unit | Cumulated quantity | Cumulated activation | Periodic quantity | Periodic activation
CPD	Type | Object | Description | Var, plan costs per acty. Unit per period | Fixed plan costs per period | Var. plan qty. per acty. Unit per period | Fixed plan qty. per period | Activation condition
CPI	Type | Object | Description | Plan costs per period | Planned quantity per period | Activation condition
PAC	Type | Description | Object | Unit | Plan quantity | Plan activation | Actual quantity | Actual activation
PCA	Type | Object | Description | Plan amount per period | Planned quantity per period | Unit | Activation condition
SBP	Type | Description | Object | Activation | Unit | Plan: Variable quantity factor | Plan: Fixed quantity per period | Actual: Variable quantity factor | Actual: Fixed quantity per period
SCD	Type | Description | Object | Activation | Unit | Plan: Variable quantity factor | Plan: Fixed quantity per period | Actual: Variable quantity factor | Actual: Fixed quantity per period
SCI	Type | Description | Object | Activation | Unit | Plan: Fixed quantity per period | Actual: Fixed quantity per period

Environment	Column Types
SKD	Type | Object | Description | Actual quantity | Actual activation
SKI	Type | Object | Description | Actual quantity | Actual activation
SOP	Type | Object | Description | Unit | Plan quantity | Plan activation

Table 7.6: Columns by environment

7.6 Template transactions

There are many transactions that are associated with template allocations. These lists are broken down by template application to make it easy to determine which transactions apply to specific functions. Some transactions show up in more than one list. The relevant environments for each transaction are listed the tables, where applicable. Table 7.7 lists the transactions used for creating and maintaining templates.

Trans	Description	Purpose
CPT1	Create template	Non-ECP environments only
CPT2	Change template	Non-ECP environments only
CPT3	Display template	Non-ECP environments only
CPT4	Delete template	Non-ECP environments only
CKCM	Costing Model	Environments 200—215 only
CTU6	Function Tree: Tree Control	Configuration—maintain environments and function trees

Table 7.7: Template maintenance transactions

The COB application is associated with orders and cost estimates. Table 7.8 lists transactions for this application.

Trans	Description	Purpose
CPTA	Actual Template Allocation: Order	Actual allocations for a single order—environments 001, 007—012

226

Trans	Description	Purpose
CPTB	Actual Template Allocation: Orders	Actual allocations for multiple internal orders—environment 007
CPTD	Actual Template Alloc: Prod. Orders	Actual allocations for multiple manufacturing orders—environments 001, 009—012
CPTE	Actual Template Alloc.: Run Sched.	Actual allocations for a single product cost collector—environment 010
CPTG	Actual Templ. Allocation: Cost Obj.	Actual allocations for a single cost object—environment 006
CPTH	Actual Templ. Allocation: Cost Obj.	Actual allocations for multiple cost objects—environment 006
CPTJ	Actl Template Allocation: Cust. Orders	Actual allocations for multiple sales orders– environment 008
CPTK	Actual Template Allocation: Project	Actual allocations for a single project, WBS element, or network—environments 004 and 005
CPTL	Actual Template Allocation: Projects	Actual allocations for multiple projects, WBS elements, or networks—environments 004 and 005
CPUA	Plan Template Allocation: Order	Plan allocations for a single order—environments 006, 007
CPUB	Plan Template Allocation: Orders	Plan allocations for multiple orders– environments 006, 007
CPUK	Plan Template Allocation: Project	Plan allocations for a single project, WBS element, or network—environments 004 and 005
CPUL	Plan Template Allocation: Projects	Plan allocations for multiple projects, WBS elements, or networks—environments 004 and 005
CK11N	Create Material Cost Estimate	Plan allocations—environment 001
CK51N	Create Order BOM Cost Estimate	Plan allocations—environment 008
KKE1	Add Base Planning Object	Plan allocations—environment 002

Trans	Description	Purpose
KKE2	Change Base Planning Object	Plan allocations—environment 002
CKUC	Multilevel Unit Costing	Plan allocations—environment 003
KTPF	View Maint.: Find Template	Configuration for assignment of an overhead key to the template

Table 7.8: COB application transactions

Easy Cost Planning uses its own set of transactions, shown in Table 7.9, that are not used by the other template environments.

Trans	Description	Purpose
CKCM	Costing Model	Environments 200—215 only
CKECP	Ad Hoc Cost Estimate	Ad hoc cost estimate
CJ9ECP	Project System: Easy Cost Planning	Create cost estimate for projects
CKECPCP	Ad Hoc Cost Estimate for cProjects	Create cost estimate for cProjects

Table 7.9: ECP application transactions

Formula planning uses templates to plan costs for cost centers and business process. The relevant transactions are in Table 7.10.

Trans	Description	Purpose
CPT6	Formula Plan for Bus. Processes	Plan allocation for business processes—environment BPP
KPT6	Execute Formula Planning	Plan allocation for cost centers— environments CSD and CSI
KS01	Create cost center	Assign template to cost center
KS02	Change cost center	Assign template to cost center
CP01	Create Business Process	Assign template to business process
CP02	Change Business Process	Assign template to business process

Table 7.10: CPI application transactions

The SBP application templates are used for actual and plan allocations for cost centers and business processes. The transactions associated with this are in Table 7.11.

Trans	Description	Purpose
CPAS	Act. Template Alloc. Bus. Processes	Actual allocations for business processes—environment SBP
CPPS	Plan Template Allocation: Process	Plan allocations for business processes—environment SBP
KPAS	Actl. Templ. Alloc: CCTR/Acty Type	Actual allocations for cost centers / activity types—environments SCD and SCI
KPPS	Allocation Templ. Plan: CCtr/Atyp	Plan allocations for cost centers / activity types—environments SCD and SCI
KS01	Create cost center	Assign template to cost center
KS02	Change cost center	Assign template to cost center
CP01	Create Business Process	Assign template to business process
CP02	Change Business Process	Assign template to business process

Table 7.11: SBP application transactions

Actual and plan statistical key figure allocations to cost centers use a separate specific application. The transactions involved with the SKI application are in Table 7.12.

Trans	Description	Purpose
KSSK	Temp. Alloc. Actual: Stat. Key Figure	Actual allocations for statistical key figures—environments SKD and SKI
KS01	Create cost center	Assign template to cost center
KS02	Change cost center	Assign template to cost center

Table 7.12: SKI application transactions

Profit center accounting uses templates for formula planning. The PCA application transactions are in Table 7.13.

Trans	Description	Purpose
7KET	Execute Formula Planning	Actual allocations for profit center formula planning—environment PCA
KE51	Create Profit Center	Assign template to profit center
KE52	Change Profit Center	Assign template to profit center

Table 7.13: PCA application transactions

Templates are used for actual allocations to Costing-Based CO-PA and are found in the PAC application. Table 7.14 outlines the pertinent transactions.

Trans	Description	Purpose
CPAE	Actl. Template Alloc: Prof. Analysis	Actual allocations for CO-PA—environment PAC
CPPE	Plan Templ. Alloc.: Results Analysis	Plan allocations for CO-PA—environment PAC
KEAE	Generate Proc. Template Environment	Configuration to generate the template environment for costing based CO-PA
KEAS	Selection Characteristics CO-PA/ABC	Configuration to specify characteristics for template allocation
KEKW	Maintain Process Template Determin.	Configuration for CO-PA template determination and other update characteristics
KEVG	Record Types for Process Costs	Configuration for record types for selecting cost drivers

Table 7.14: PAC application transactions

When transferring the sales and operations plan, templates can be used for allocations. These are processed using the SOP application, and the transactions are found in Table 7.15.

Trans	Description	Purpose
KSOP	CO-OM-ABC: Transfer SOP/LTP	Plan allocations for sales and operation plan—environment SOP
KTPF	View Maint.: Find Template	Configuration for assignment of an overhead key to the template

Table 7.15: SOP application transactions

SEM Banking can use templates for allocations to CO-PA. Transactions associated with the ISB application are found in Table 7.16.

Trans	Description	Purpose
JBKW	Actual Process Allocation: Fin. Obj.	Actual allocations—environments BAC, BCD, BKK, BLN, BSO, BSS, BST, BSV, BVT
JBT1	Maintain Costing Rule	Configuration—connection of the template
JBPD	Update Character. for Process Costs	Configuration—definition of characteristics for allocation to CO-PA

Table 7.16: ISB application transactions

7.7 CKF_RES_TPL fields

Structure CKF_RES_TPL is used in Easy Cost Planning to enable objects to be assigned in model characteristics at the time the cost estimate is created. The list of fields is found in Table 7.17.

Field	Description	Data Type	Length
TYPPS	Item category	CHAR	1
KOKRS_HRK	Origin controlling area item	CHAR	4
EXTNR	Base planning object	CHAR	18
KOSTL	Cost center	CHAR	10
LSTAR	Activity type	CHAR	6
MATNR	Material number	CHAR	18
WERKS	Plant	CHAR	4
PSCHL	Pricing key	CHAR	18
ASNUM	Activity number	CHAR	18
INFNR	Purchasing info record number	CHAR	10
EKORG	Purchasing organization	CHAR	4
PRZNR	Business process	CHAR	12
BWTAR	Valuation type	CHAR	10
LIFNR	Vendor/creditor account number	CHAR	10
KSTAR	Cost element	CHAR	10
LTEXT	Description	CHAR	40
MODEL	Costing Model	CHAR	10
LPREIS	Price in Entry Currency	CURR	15.2
LPREIFX	Fixed Price in Entry Currency	CURR	15.2
WAERS	Currency Key	CUKY	5
BUPER	Posting Period	NUMC	3
VERWS	Reference of KALKTAB Items to a Context	CHAR	35
INFNR_F	Purchasing Info Record Number—External Processing	CHAR	10
KSTAR_V	Cost Element	CHAR	10
MEEHT	Base Unit of Measure	CHAR	3
TPLCLASS	Template Environment	CHAR	3

Table 7.17: Fields in structure CKF_RES_TPL

ESPRESSO TUTORIALS

You have finished the book.

A   The Author

Tom King is a graduate of Northwestern University and is currently a Senior Business Analyst at Milliken and Company, a US-based manufacturer of textiles, floor coverings, and chemicals. His involvement with SAP systems began in 2007, when Milliken began converting its legacy systems to ECC 6.0. Previously, he helped design and configure the Activity Based Costing implementation in Milliken's European operations. He has also written an article for Financial Experts and has presented at the ASUG and Controlling conferences.

B Index

C Disclaimer

This publication contains references to the products of SAP SE.

SAP, R/3, SAP NetWeaver, Duet, PartnerEdge, ByDesign, SAP BusinessObjects Explorer, StreamWork, and other SAP products and services mentioned herein as well as their respective logos are trademarks or registered trademarks of SAP SE in Germany and other countries.

Business Objects and the Business Objects logo, BusinessObjects, Crystal Reports, Crystal Decisions, Web Intelligence, Xcelsius, and other Business Objects products and services mentioned herein as well as their respective logos are trademarks or registered trademarks of Business Objects Software Ltd. Business Objects is an SAP company.

Sybase and Adaptive Server, iAnywhere, Sybase 365, SQL Anywhere, and other Sybase products and services mentioned herein as well as their respective logos are trademarks or registered trademarks of Sybase, Inc. Sybase is an SAP company.

SAP SE is neither the author nor the publisher of this publication and is not responsible for its content. SAP Group shall not be liable for errors or omissions with respect to the materials. The only warranties for SAP Group products and services are those that are set forth in the express warranty statements accompanying such products and services, if any. Nothing herein should be construed as constituting an additional warranty.

More Espresso Tutorials Books

Thomas Michael:

Reporting for SAP® Asset Accounting

- ▶ Basic asset accounting reporting features
- ▶ Balance, transaction and specialtity reports
- ▶ Asset history sheet and US tax reporting

http://5029.espresso-tutorials.com

Tanya Duncan:

Practical Guide to SAP® CO-PC (Product Cost Controlling)

- ▶ Cost Center Planning Process and Costing Run Execution
- ▶ Actual Cost Analysis & Reporting
- ▶ Controlling Master Data
- ▶ Month End Processes in Details

http://5064.espresso-tutorials.com

Ashish Sampat:

First Steps in SAP® Controlling (CO)

▶ Cost center and product cost planning and actual cost flow

▶ Best practices for cost absorption using Product Cost Controlling

▶ Month-end closing activities in SAP Controlling

▶ Examples and screenshots based on a case study approach

http://5069.espresso-tutorials.com

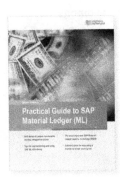

Rosana Fonseca:

Practical Guide to SAP® Material Ledger (ML)

▶ SAP Material Ledger functionality and key integration points

▶ Tips for implementing and using SAP ML effectively

▶ The most important SAP Material Ledger reports, including CKM3N

▶ Detailed steps for executing a multilevel actual costing run

http://5116.espresso-tutorials.com

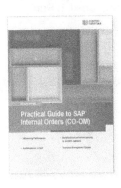

Marjorie Wright:

Practical Guide to SAP® Internal Orders (CO-OM)

▶ Concepts and daily postings to internal orders

▶ Master data configuration

▶ Streamlining period-end close activities

▶ Reporting options and summarization hierarchies in SAP CO

http://5139.espresso-tutorials.com

Ashish Sampat:

Expert Tips to Unleash the Full Potential of SAP® Controlling

- ▶ Optimize SAP ERP Controlling configuration, reconciliation, and reporting
- ▶ Transaction processiong tips to ensure accurate data capture
- ▶ Instructions for avoiding common month-end close pain points
- ▶ Reporting and reconciliation best practices

http://5140.espresso-tutorials.com

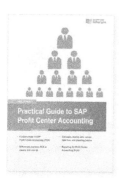

John Pringle:

Practical Guide to SAP® Profit Center Accounting

- ▶ Fundamentals of SAP Profit Center Accounting (PCA)
- ▶ Concepts, master data, actual data flow, and planning basics
- ▶ Differences between PCA in classic and new GL
- ▶ Reporting for Profit Center Accounting (PCA)

http://5144.espresso-tutorials.com

Janet Salmon & Claus Wild:

First Steps in SAP® S/4HANA Finance

- ▶ Understand the basics of SAP S/4HANA Finance
- ▶ Explore the new architecture, configuration options, and SAP Fiori
- ▶ Examine SAP S/4HANA Finance migration steps
- ▶ Assess the impact on business processes

http://5149.espresso-tutorials.com

Stefan Eifler, Christoph Theis:

Value Flows into SAP® ERP FI, CO and CO-PA

▶ Value flows based on the sales and production processes

▶ Reconciliation between FI and CO-PA

▶ Overhead costs and closing tasks

▶ Overview of SAP S/4 HANA Finance

http://5199.espresso-tutorials.com